What's Cooking on the Isle of Wight

and

The Wight Good Food Guide

★ ★ ★ ⊥

by

Angela Hewitt

Of the former renowned Lugley's Restaurant

Travelling
Gourmet
Publications

Third Edition 2007
ISBN 13: 978-0-9521697-4-1
Text and images © Angela Hewitt

British Library Cataloguing in Publication Data
A catalogue record for this book is available from the British Library

Details are correct at the time of going to press

Other books by Angela Hewitt:

Cooking on the Move
Herb Growers Recipe Book
Isle of Wight Cookery
What's Cooking in Brighton
What's Cooking in the Cotswolds
What's Cooking on the Isle of Wight, Editions 1 and 2
What's Cooking in the New Forest
What's Cooking in Oxford

Travelling Gourmet Publications
Padmore Lodge, Beatrice Avenue, East Cowes, Isle of Wight, PO32 6LP
Tel/Fax: (44) 01983 296110 email: angela.hewitt@btclick.com
www.angelahewitt.co.uk

to Roger
he keeps my feet on the ground

★★★★★

The Author Angela Hewitt

I have lived on the Isle of Wight for 35 years and as a lover of eating out I have eaten in almost every establishment on the Island. I was chef proprietor of the former renowned Lugley's (TM) Restaurant from 1980-1994. It won awards from Egon Ronay, The Good Food Guide, AA Good Food Guide, and Michelin. I closed the restaurant 12 years ago, basically due to sheer exhaustion. Over the subsequent years I have written Isle of Wight Cookery published by Dovecote Press and What's Cooking on the Isle of Wight, published by Travelling Gourmet Publications. I also wrote, What's Cooking In Oxford, What's Cooking in the New Forest, What's Cooking in Brighton, What's Cooking in the Cotswolds, Cooking on the Move and Herb Growers Cookery.

I love to promote the Island— my little piece of paradise— whenever I can so I was delighted to be asked by various TV production companies to appear in their programmes promoting the island. This included promoting Isle of Wight garlic with Simon Broom from Blue Peter who was doing a tour of Foody England. Another garlic promotion which turned into a bit of a farce albeit great fun, was with TV cook Susan Brooks from the Richard and Judy Good Morning programme. I had to make garlic ice-cream, little knowing that she was going to doctor her version of it (masses of garlic) to feed to the poor old Book Club couple.

I have also written food articles for Taste Magazine, Healthy Eating Magazine, Taste of Britain Magazine and Trailfinders.

I am now a full-time artist and greeting card producer but I still find time to promote the Island and, good cooking by offering advice based on my knowledge of running Lugley's restaurant whenever I can, hence this food guide and cookery book.

4

CONTENTS

**The Wight Good Food Guide
Sponsors of
The Rotary Chefs of the Year Competition**

Wight Good Food Guide

T his guide is totally independent. It receives no sponsorship, advertising, discounts or any other kind of benefits. All meals are paid for in full by myself—including meals that are not mentioned in this guide. The aim of this guide is to support good Island cooking and to encourage all eateries to step up to the plate what ever kind of food they are selling to the public. It also aims to promote the use of good British produce, in particular to encourage restaurants to reflect the Isle of Wight and the seasons in its cooking and choice of menu.

Good restaurant cooking requires lots of skills. Purchasing of the right ingredients, knowledge of how to treat ingredients to extract the best from them, perfect cooking times, good marriages of flavours, an obsession and love of working with food, an ability to deal with lots of different things at once and, above all, consistency.

The Rules

A ll the reviews are my own personal opinion. Although I may visit a restaurant anonymously one has to bear in mind that the Island is a small place and word of who I may be soon gets around. I also knows that if they twig who I am it is not going to make a huge difference to the way things are cooked that night—a bad cook cannot suddenly become a good cook overnight. I do however, believe that there is always room for improvement—the more you try to do something well the better you will get.

Reviewing an eating establishment is not easy. I might just approve two of the three dishes or they may have an off day—which is basically unacceptable, but it is not my intention to be harsh. I have the skill and experience to judge potential even in the summer when kitchens are stretched and they are pushing themselves past their limit.

The Star System

No * = oddities, possibly recommending a particular dish

* A Good Start
** Getting There
*** Close to Tops
**** Top of the Bill—an all rounder, fine cooking, good ingredients, friendly, unobtrusive service, good value for money

MASTER CLASS

CREDIT CARDS

As a frequent solo diner I often feel discriminated against by establishments who will not accept cards for less than £10. My bill is frequently below this amount. Even worse, and this happened to me, my bill came to £9.55 and I was told I had to pay a surcharge of 75p which took it over £10. I hope you see the stupidity of this as much as I do?

This attitude is short-sighted and terrible customer service. One restaurant told me that customers were quite happy to go to the cash point after a meal and draw out money (presumably even in the rain) and that they had had no complaints—I told them that they had had a complaint—from me. A pub that worries about the loss of a few pence in card charges is losing a great deal more than a few pence. It is losing future custom.

BEMBRIDGE

Fultons Seafood and Chop House ★+

This relaxed chop house offers a large choice of interesting dishes which means perfection is not the easiest thing on the menu. However, the basic menu hasn't changed which allows for execution to be honed.

They specialise in fresh fish and there is an open display cabinet where I am sure they would let you choose your catch of the day. I decided this time to choose from the standard menu. My natural smoked haddock came cooked just right with a superb, smooth and creamy mashed potato and a light, creamy wholegrain mustard sauce. A simple straight forward dish cooked to perfection.

My dessert was Cuban passion fruit trifle. It looked huge and full of crème chantilly, custard and the usual trifle ingredients. Having decided that I would not eat it all I was amazed to find myself scraping the dish clean.

Fultons is a hard edged trendy cafe bar but the chairs are comfortable and the wood soft. The art on the walls is exceptional and tells you the proprietors understand quality and style.

The service is exceptionally friendly albeit a little slow on busy days, which is great if you are not in a hurry. *Phone 01983 875559*

BONCHURCH

The Pond Café **+

The Pond has a nice atmosphere, formal trendy on the inside and casual on the roadside patio—great for summer eating.

The new chef is settling in nicely and is offering gourmet cuisine with a bistro style rusticity. I took my maddish Mum for her birthday dinner. We thoroughly enjoyed ham and foie gras terrine, pan seared tuna on a bed of Mediterranean salad with feta cheese. I was surprised how the combination of feta and tuna married so well. This was followed by properly char-grilled rib eye steak that had been flattened with a mallet in the French style served with wonderful tempura vegetables. My salmon was pan fried to perfection and served on a bed of dainty samphire, (botanically known as glasswort). The accompanying vegetables were al denté (al denté means cooked just right with a slight bite—it does not mean crunchy). Desserts are simple. My fresh fruit salad was fairly ordinary but the accompanying yoghurt and lime sorbet was really very good. Mum had the pecan and pine-nut tart with a rich textured salt butter ice cream. We were suspicious that the tart was bought in but were assured by the staff hat it wasn't.
Phone 01983 855666

Bonchurch Inn *

This is not just a step back in time but a leap into another world. The small bar at Bonchurch Inn reeks of nostalgia. Pubs when pubs were real pubs not family eateries. Old men sat around a crib table, ladies in felt hats with their glass of stout in an atmosphere that is dark, quiet and restful. The courtyard entrance tells a different tale of Provincial France, where an ancient stone walled alley leads to a hideaway known only to the locals.

The Inn is run by an Italian family steeped in tradition. A few basic dishes such as scampi and chips are available for those frightened of food. Then a typical Anglo/Italian menu with little embellishment lists lasagne, spaghetti Bolognaise, pasta carbonara, and pizza.

There are certain dishes that I never order unless I am confident they are genuinely home-made and of some quality, such as pizza. The pizza at Bonchurch Inn is a must. The base is tender and freshly baked, not like the hard defrosted rubbish you get in most places and the tomato and cheese topping is intensely flavoured. I took the "Brawn" with me. He had the Anti-pasto Platter, packed with meat and other delicacies. Stick with the Italian dishes.

In the winter cuddle up in the tiny bar and on a hot summer's day chill out in the courtyard. By the way, beer comes from the barrel.
Phone 01983 852611

COWES

Mojacs Restaurant *

The décor may need upgrading to reflect today's penitent for the hard edges that create a vibrant canteen atmosphere, but the food is very good.

We, the Brawn and I enjoyed pink chicken livers (as they should be) in a cream sauce, and an exceptionally well cooked confit of duck under a filo pastry lid—slow cooked to a tenderness that made it melt in the mouth. The pork belly main course was perhaps a bit full on and heavy going but my fish in coconut sauce was spot on. Vegetables were fresh and al denté.

The food is rather rich and filling and sauces tend to swamp the dishes. If I had not been doing a review I would have forsaken a pudding. I did however go for a chocolate bavarois—a kind of proper blancmange served in its simples form. *Phone: 01983 281118*

EAST COWES

Albert Cottage *

I have a confession to make, I have a prejudice, which is, I am not keen on formal dining room eating. I think it tempers personalities and diners never look as if they are really enjoying themselves, best behaviour and all that! Formality is what Albert Cottage is all about. However, there is a curious walk to the restaurant along a long, long, tunnel like corridor and the dining room is friendlier than most. My Sunday lunch was very good. Pink freshly carved beef, home-made Yorkshire although I think the batter may have been a little too thick, proper roast potatoes and perfect pan juice gravy not the flour thickened stuff you get at most places. The choice of starters are simple and un-adventurous. I had pears with crumbled stilton, walnuts, dressing and leaves. My version would be a pear stuffed with roqueforte cream, coated in sour cream dressing and garnished with leaves with honeygar dressing and toasted pinenuts. The dessert was perfectly executed, panna cotta—all the rage these days—(getting boooring...) with hot caramelised pineapple and toffee sauce. The evening menu looks interesting.
Phone 01983 299309

The Terrace Restaurant at Osborne House *

The Terrace dining room is a relaxed dinning room catering for an onslaught of tourists in the most elegant way possible. Beautiful white plaster cornices, stained glass window, contemporary lighting, polished floor boards and even with dark chocolate brown walls is light, airy and uplifting. All food is cold apart from the soup which I was informed was served warm. My chicken liver pâté with a little chutney was as it should be, fresh, home-made and tasty. I went for the vegetarian option main course a three bean cheesecake, fine beans, broad beans and runner beans accompanied with more-beans salad. This would have been a more successful dish if accompanied with a sauce, maybe sour cream or blue cheese or simply a dollop of home-made mayonnaise. My glass of Adgeston white wine was a perfect accompaniment for a light, cold lunch. My dessert of lemon and lime posset was inspired. It came with buttery, crumble shortbread and a few sweet strawberries and was the star dish. Considering the food is cold it wasn't cheap plus, if you are not a member of English heritage there is an entrance fee of £5.50.
Phone 01983 298052

FRESHWATER

Apple Tree Café at Afton Park * +

Wendy the chef clearly respects perfectly fresh ingredients—a lesson for many would be chefs can be found here. I popped in for a quick snack, saw the still stiff mackerel and couldn't resist. She lightly coated it in flour and gently pan fried it until it was really crisp on the outside and well cooked—as mackerel should be—on the inside. She served it with fab bread made with Island wheat from the local bakery and a wedge of lemon, no sauce no garnish just simple excellence on a plate.

Their menu is short and interesting, nettle soup, rustic breads, own recipe gluten free scones, own made pickles and chutneys to go with own made pâtés. They promote Island sausages, Island rare breeds beef, local chickens and duck. However, it is the cooking that makes these ingredients stand out. To drink I had their own-brew apple juice. I overheard the proprietor tell a customer that it was made from Bramley and Cox apples with slightly more Cox than Bramley to give it a natural sweetness. *Phone 01983 755774*

The Red Lion *

It was a warm winter's day when I visited this old pub next to Freshwater church. Just arriving in the area makes you feel as if you have entered a world of traditional village life. If a coach and horses drove past you wouldn't blink.

The friendly barman was eager to serve and patient to wait while I read through the wide ranging miss-spelt menu offering wonderful country style dishes with various game and fresh fish suggestions. They offer something for every taste. I have eaten here several times and have enjoyed venison, pickled walnut and ale pie was really a casserole with a separately cooked pastry crust, (this is a great idea if you like your pastry light and crisp, but not if you like the flavour of the gravy to seep into the pastry while it is cooking) also pheasant in game stock based brandy sauce. Vegetables come as a large selection which are not only interesting but perfectly cooked. Desserts are mainly traditional with the odd unusual offering such as raspberry and Cointreau bruleé or ginger and whisky trifle. I detect a few acceptable short cuts regarding ingredients. Food portions are generous and sourcing of ingredients usually good.

The pub is broken up into little alcoves, giving a feeling of intimacy and privacy. Soft wooden floors, scrubbed tables and gentle lighting was a bit like cross dressing—an old fashioned farmhouse kitchen dressed up as a trendy country pub. *Phone 01983 754925*

GODSHILL

The Essex *** Best State of the Art Restaurant 2007

Recently while out cycling I decided to pop in for lunch. The beams are painted white, the patterned carpet replaced with pine floorboards and the walls painted a soft peach. The chairs are tall-backed leather and the tables are covered with pristine white clothes and real starched napkins.

I was the only diner but later a couple from London turned up—looking for a hearty meal.

There were two set lunch menus and I could have eaten any of it, it all sounded delicious. I chose a starter of smoked haddock and smoked salmon with a cheese and mustard sauce. I was assured it was not too rich as their sauces were delicate. The Brawn always say delicate means tasteless and I tend to agree with him. The reason this dish was not too rich albeit very tasty was that it was so small, the size of a large canapé. If the starter was the size of a canapé the main course was the size of a starter. It was however, excellent. Little squares of sea-bass nicely cooked on a bed of fresh crushed new potatoes and buttery curly kale. The accompanying vanilla sauce (jus, pronounced ju) was highly unusual and really nice and, a true sauce reduction, tiny roasted onions made an appropriate garnish. The best bit was the pudding, coconut parfait, mango sorbet, kaffir lime leaf panna cotta and a coconut tuile finished with a lacy, drizzle of syrup.

Service was excellent with constant reassurances that food was on its way. A necessary requirement when everything is cooked to order. (I accept that good food takes time—not everyone does). I did worry about the London couple though, I hope they got enough to eat.

I returned a few weeks later for dinner. It was marvellous and included lots of little magical freebies between courses. I will always remember the dessert which was hot chocolate beignetts.

The Essex supports the use of local ingredients and list their suppliers with a short biography at the back of the menu—well done.
Phone 01983 840232

For regular updated restaurant reviews go to www.angelahewitt.co.uk

NEWPORT

Burrs **+

This little Bistro, once the Tap at the back of the Bugle Hotel—do any of you remember that? has great atmosphere. It reminds me of one of those back street Parisian cafes full of Gitanè smoke and accordion music. The majority of Burr's dishes are home cooked. The scallops in my starter were grilled to perfection—tender and creamy on the inside, the chilli sauce tasted like the one I get from my specialist Indonesian deli on the mainland. My main course was a success with juicy pink slices of duck breast served with cherry sauce. Of course at the time cherries were out of season so they probably came out of the freezer but the sticky sauce was a true reduction. My strudel was only spoilt by the fact it was reheated in the microwave so the pastry became soggy. This was compensated for and all was forgiven with the complimentary home-made wholemeal and date bread—excellent stuff.

On a second visit I enjoyed amazing puff balls in garlic and creamy and tangy raspberry cheeses cake.

Phone 01983 825470

Quay Arts Café *

The food is exactly the kind of food one would expect to be offered in an art centre. Healthy, salads, the SOD (soup of day) is normally vegetable, quiche, vegetarian terrines, baguettes using wholemeal bread - an improvement on the white variety served everywhere else—jackets and home made cakes. They also offer meat and fish dishes.

The cafe is quite dark but the outside deck on the bank of the Medina river is a pleasant place to sit.

it is a favourite place of mine a visit to the gallery followed by a cup of tea and a piece of date slice. It can get very busy during the lunchtime - even during the Winter so be prepared to queue. *Phone 01983 822490*

Be aware that some establishments make a service charge on payment by credit card if you do not spend enough

MASTER CLASS

A BRACE OF PHEASANTS

The season for pheasant shooting commences on the 1st October and ends 1st February. However, because the weather on the Island is milder in comparison with the rest of the country, the open season tends to start a couple of weeks later.

The biggest question regarding pheasant is *'To hang or not to hang?!'* . . ..And the next question *'For how long?'*. The answers should be based on how cold the weather is and how high you like your bird to be.

The idea of hanging (that is a piece of cord tied around the dead bird's neck and hung while still in feather in a cool, dry, airy place at about 0-5°C), is to allow the flesh to relax. The enzymes in the flesh begin to chemically break down the meat, thus tenderizing it and giving it its characteristic 'gamey' taste. In fact most pheasant will be only six months old when shot tenderizing isn't really necessary, and as it has a unique and delicious flavour anyway, to achieve a 'gamey' flavour is different but not essential.

A pheasant that is 'high' is the stage just before 'off'. Depending on the weather it can happen at any time between 12 hours and 6 days after shooting. Pheasant is 'off' when its flesh begins to turn a rather unpleasant green. During the warm month of October, and often November, it is probably best not to hang any longer then overnight, and during the colder weather no more than 4 days.

Usually sold by the brace, one female hen and one male cock, it amounts to an economical meal. The male is bigger and meatier than the smaller, but more tender, female. To check for age, look at the pointed spur just above the feet at the back of the leg. The spur of an old bird will be large, dark and more pointed than a young one. Pheasant is one of the easiest birds to pluck and a satisfying thing to do. It's worth having a go.

11

Olivo Restaurant *

It is a tricky business putting on a roast special all day. Do you cook one large joint and reheat it for the end of day orders or cook smaller joints at intervals throughout the day? How a restaurant handles this is testing—will it end up like reheated school dinners. Olivo did it like this... Cook fresh vegetables to tender perfection. Place while piping hot on plate. Lay on top nicely cooked cold slices of pork stuffed with parma ham and fennel seeds. Pour over hot, rich beer flavoured gravy. To my enjoyment it worked! The pork was tender, moist and of good texture. It gives me pleasure to see such thought put into the presentation of what I consider to be a challenging dish.

My starter of deep fried calamari with spicy chickpea cream dressing was very good and my dessert showed and understanding of flavours. The fruit terrine was red berries set in a clear aspic. It was fruity and sharp and not drowning in sugary jelly, the white chocolate ice-cream was a good accompaniment and the presentation delightfully simple.

Unlike many establishments they nearly always get their cappucino right. It's a third, a third, a third! *Phone 01983 520002*

Gods Providence House *

Life can be full of disappointments. For me it is going to a restaurant that I originally thought was good only to find on another visit, the chef has changed along with the quality of the cooking—for the worst! This means that the one thing I am always looking for is consistency. Whether the establishment is chef/proprietor based or the chef is employed, the quality of the cooking is the responsibility of the owner not the chef. I have been eating in Gods Providence tearooms for over 20 years and they are as consistent as ever. Things have subtly changed, for instance the coconut and chocolate slice has vanished as has the upstairs salad bar. I am sad about this as I had many girly lunches up there 20 years ago. But we must move on. They still serve wholemeal pastry quiche with a selection of salads. I remember the grated carrot and coconut salad with great affection. Gods Providence is now onto it's fourth owner and they have the same sense as those before, if it works don't change it.

Gods providence is the nearest one can get to tinkling teacups and oldé world charm, and old fashioned pre-war food—comfort food. Steak Pie and Steak pudding, with a selection of well cooked vegetables, poached egg on toast, omelettes, scones, egg mayonnaise sandwiches, fruit jelly and lemon meringue pie. Their concession to the modern world is cafetiére coffee selection, herbal teas and BLT; and now some delicious looking puddings. Waitresses in black and white uniforms are quick and friendly.

Phone 01983 522085

MASTER CLASS

SUNDAY LUNCH

In the home Sunday lunch is served at the same time to everyone. This guarantees an almost perfect meal. Beautifully cooked meat, crunchy roast potatoes, al dente vegetables etc. If you have customers turning up at different times the only way to serve a perfect Sunday lunch is to stagger the cooking to fit in with the arrival of each individual booking—cooking some 10 to 15 individual roasts—an impossibility unless you are a magician.

The Sunday Carvery was a good try but it meant soggy vegetables, crispy Yorkshires and eventually dry meat. The answer is to serve Sunday roast at a set time. The customer who likes good food will find this commendable.

RYDE

Liberty's *

Liberty's is following the current fashion of café bar society. To be honest I have been there a couple of times before, not for lunch but for a cup of coffee and their to die for forest fruits crumble tart with a little scoop of honey ice cream on the side and driddled with caramel sauce. It was so good I went back for more a couple of weeks later. This is a dangerous thing to do because consistency or rather lack of it can often let a restaurant down.

Liberty's is modern, young and easy, yet it has a kind of 'comfortable club' feel about it. The ceilings are high enough for voices to be lost in the eves.

You can wait to be served or write your order on the pad left on the table and take it to the bar. I asked one the staff about some of the dishes on offer and was impressed that she could answer me and didn't have to run back of house to ask the chef. She was also helpful when it came to suggesting a non-alcoholic lunchtime drink

The lunch menu is a good read and many of the dishes are tempting as well as recognisable. My caramelised red onion and feta cheese tartlet came warm with a little salad garnish. The pastry was crisp and melted in the mouth and the filling slightly sweet and creamy. I have also had haddock and Parma ham fishcakes with a cold tomato salsa. It was a nice combination and not too heavy. Consistency can be an issue—something that is difficult to maintain if chefs are frequently changing.

Their puddings seem to be their triumph and I nearly always go for their trio collection.
Phone 01983 811007

MASTER CLASS

CHIPS

What happened to them?! All of a sudden we are being given fat "chips", chunky "chips", extra big "chips", in fact chips that are not chips at all. Fat chips just do not work—a chip has an optimum size—for a reason. It has to be deep fried in hot fat so that it is soft and fluffy on the inside and not burnt on the outside and fat chips will urn before they are cooked.Still on chips, if a high achieving restaurant serving bought in chips, uses the excuse of "too busy to make them" during lunch time trade then they should not be on the menu. Even Jireh House in Yarmouth cooks their own chips!

MASTER CLASS

PERFECT CRÈME BRULÉE

To one litre of double cream add 7 egg yolks in the Spring when yolks are seasonally rich and 8 yolks the rest of the year. Add 1-2 oz sugar and the seeds scraped from a vanilla pod.

Pour mixture into individual ramekins or cups and place in a roasting tin of water (bain marie). Cover with tin foil and cook in the oven for 1 hour. Cool, then dredge the surface lightly with castor sugar and perhaps for a few finely grated strands of orange peel with sugar.

Then either put under fiercely hot grill to melt the sugar or blast with a blow torch.

SEAVIEW

Priory Hotel Restaurant ★★

I popped into the Priory for lunch without a booking mid week. There was a conference on so I was sat in one of the reception rooms made up as a temporary dining room.

My wild mushroom risotto starter was excellent. The grain aldenté and perfectly balanced with the creaminess of the other ingredients. This with side salad would make and excellent lunch in itself. This was followed by salmon coated in sesame seeds and oven baked. The texture of the salmon was moist and slightly pink in the middle—just how it should be, it did however, need more sauce. The vegetables came in a separate bowl and I scoffed the lot. The pudding I chose was a little Baked Alaska. Although strictly speaking it wasn't baked as the meringue topping wasn't set all the way through, but browned on the surface with either a welding torch or under the grill. All the same it was very nice. I have also enjoyed dinner, this time in the bar which looked more cosy than the restaurant.

Priory Oyster ★

It is easy to be beguiled by the surroundings, which are perfect for eating alfresco on a hot sunny day or balmy evening. Although I was told booking is essential it is a hugely casual place to eat and the back bone of cooking is the Bar B Que. A good BBQ is not just a case of "chucking something on the barby" and waiting for it all to be ready at the same time. Timing is crucial and how long it takes for something to cook on an open flame is essential knowledge if you do not want burnt, dry, overcooked offerings. The perfect BBQ'd ingredient will be charred on the outside and succulent inside. The Priory Oyster kitchen is a shack in the woods above the Priory Bay beach. The cafe is on a raised wooden platform with sea glimpses through the trees. I went with a girl friend and we kept it simple. We shared a starter of Bruchetta with to-mato concasse. We then ordered the BBQ sea bass and BBQ sardines. They came with salad garnish and bought-in French fries and by way of contradiction the best mayonnaise I have had this year, rich and tasty with the sublime flavour of fruity olive oil. The bass was cooked just so, but the sardines were on the dry side. The dessert, of chocolate mousse was good and choco-laty and was in fact a rich, chocolate truffle.

Seaview Hotel Restaurant ★★+

The restaurant at the rear is very blue and very cool, great after a hot day in the Summer sun - if we get any this year! The Brawn came despite it being a dinning room type restaurant and not bistro style. The menu gets straight to the point when it comes to cost. Starters it says are "Six pounds fifty pence" then it lists an interesting choice of what you get for £6.50. I chose Spi-der crab risotto with foam—very nice. The Brawn was intrigued by the mackerel with warm cu-cumber jelly and garnished with micro salad and horeseradish. The jelly was indeed warm but was more affectation than flavour packed and they forgot the horseradish.

Main courses the menu says are "Sixteen pounds ninety five pence" I had the black bream with toasted rice water—yes, I really did say toasted rice water which like the cucumber jelly was more affectation than flavour packed. The Brawn had some minute duck breast on a bed of parsnips drizzled with an intense reduction.

My citrus pudding was the best part a warm, syrupy, caramelised orange thingy, a fabulously tangy lime sorbet and a delightfully smooth lemon cream. The Brawn who absolutely loves all things rhubarb went for the trio of rhubarb mousse, sorbet and milk shake, the only inedible item was the straw in the shake.

A couple of freebies were thrown in—an amusé bouché (amusing the mouth) at the beginning which was a spectacular chicken live pithivier with a perfect stock reduction sauce and a pre pudding banana cake with orange sauce—slightly disappointing. With half a bottle of wine, some sparkling water it was excellent value for money. The new chef needs to look towards consistency and strong gimmick-less flavours throughout and I am sure he will be on the way to a Michelin star. Service was efficient and professional without being starchy.
Phone 01983 612711

SHANKLIN

Saffrons Restaurant *

This little bistro offers an eclectic mix of dishes which suggests the chef is by and large offering the kind of food he likes to eat. I take this as a good sign—the chef is cooking from the heart. With good sourcing of ingredients and a little more confidence in cooking times this chef is on the way to perfection.

For instance my asparagus wrapped in parma ham was a gnats too crunchy, while the poached egg that came with it was perfectly cooked but would have been nicer if it was a dainty pullet egg or a quails egg. Pork is the most difficult meat to cook as it goes from tender to hard in a split second. The pork in my pork and mozzarella cheese stack was just about right but would have been better if it had come from a younger pig. (do not buy pork that has no rind on it because this is the give away to the age of a pig). My side salad was a pleasure and came with a little jug of dressing and was much nicer than those horrible spiky rocket leave restaurants seem to be obsessed with. I have no idea why rocket leave are like this—the ones I grow at home are delicious and tender.

I enjoyed the white chocolate and red berry brulée, but a brulée is supposed to be a rich custard made with egg yolks and double cream - one of my most favourite puds. As an aside I can never understand how you can have a crab or any other kind of savoury brulée.

I loved the flat screen of changing art.
Phone 01983 862609

Morgans Restaurant *

The decor is brand spanking new and needs to be worn in for extra comfort. The menu has grown since last year. I have real problems making decisions when it comes to eating out. Not so much what do I want but more a case of what am I going to miss.

Again I hadn't booked and the staff were pleasant and efficient. Fine, no problem where would you like to sit. I like that, no fuss, no hassle, take a seat, we will be with you in a tick.

I love pâté but never have it when I eat out because I do not trust menus that say Home-made or Chefs special recipe pate only to discover that it is not homemade at all. It really annoys me because it assumes the customer is stupid. So I was pleased when I saw chefs special recipe duck liver and foie gras pâté with red onion chutney. This had to be home-made. It was indeed delicious and served in small portions due I expect to the presence of the wildly expensive foie gras. It was definitely as good as those luxuriously expensive tins of foie gras pâté I bring home from France. Catch of the day was fresh Bembridge plaice, an opportunity not to be missed. It came simply with freshly cooked vegetables—although French beans were crunchy rather than aldenté and a little dipping sauce would have made the plaice that little bit more special.

The pudding, a spicy apple crumble with custard was spoilt by the fact the custard was not proper egg custard.
Phone 01983 864900

SHORWELL

The Crown Inn *+

From a comfort point of view I prefer to sit in a "quaint old pub" rather than a stuffy restaurant but the quality of food and screaming free range children often puts me off. The pub is made up of small rooms plus a pretty outdoor garden with white doves and fat trout swimming in the stream, plus a specials board that is small enough to be copeable amidst the dross. I have to say I eat in the Crown a lot before the summer season arrives. It's the most comfortable and relaxed pub on the island with a calm atmosphere. I have enjoyed nicely cooked chicken dishes, delicious braised beef, beautifully cooked vegetables and well prepared traditional sweets.

Their Sunday roast beef is very good, the meat comes pink, carved straight off the joint and not reheated, the roast potatoes were exactly that not deep fried, the vegetables were nicely cooked and the horseradish was wonderfully firey, it was rounded off with a crisp Yorkshire pudding and tasty gravy. Service is slow but then quality was never fast. *Phone 01983 740293*

ST HELEN'S

The St Helens Restaurant ★★★★Top of the Bill 2006/7

There are times when I visit a restaurant that I find myself willing it to be good, maybe because the menu sounds interesting, the atmosphere is beguiling, the staff are friendly. The position and outlook is pleasing or they are showing an interest in where they source their ingredients. St Helens restaurant ticked all the boxes for the above list, but at the end of the day I am judging the food and the quality of cooking.

I have eaten here several times and watched it go from strength to strength, this meal was a family gathering. Despite the short menu we (Brawn, Junior Brawn and partner and me) agonised over our choices, but bagged the last Cod with crab crust from the specials menu before anyone else got it. The Brawn and one grown-up-child (GupC) declared the goat's cheese coated in pistachios and grilled to be excellent. Other GupC had posh prawn cocktail, beautifully presented and flavoursome. The mains were without exception all excellent, the cod with crab crust and my paupiettes of plaice with pesto cream both cooked to dedicated perfection. Brawn and Junior Brawn went for the pork clothed in pancetta with apple and calvados sauce and the perfectly cooked sirloin steak with good home made chips.

Only us girls managed a sweet. Female GupC chose the tender bruleé with melt in the mouth shortbread. I chose the tropical inspired panna cotta which should be tender and wobbly and slide down the throat like silk—this did exactly that. *Phone 01983 872303*

VENTNOR

Hambrough Hotel ★★★

Having peeked inside during Ventnor Jazz Festival the Brawn refused to come with me, claiming it was too stark and pretentious. In their defence I have to say that the service is really truly friendly and their whole aim is to please, plus they play great music from Billy Holiday to Kruder Dorfmeister. The music is necessary as the Hambrough is all hard edges with echos a plenty. The menu is reassuringly short, 4 starters, 4 mains and 3 puds or cheese. The up side of this is that great care can be given to the execution of each dish, the downside is with so little

16

choice it had better be good—really, really good.

My starter of cold herb rolled salmon was splendid. The tube of salmon had been poached for exactly the right length of time so that the fish was opaque all the way through, then rolled on fresh herbs. It came with a purée of blue potatoes and micro confetti of tomato.

Pork is the most difficult thing to cook, particularly fillet, as it can go from perfection to over cooked in a minute. Again it was moist and perfect (if I was cooking it I may have seared the outside to give extra flavour but this is nit-picking) the pork came with perfectly heated, well selected black pudding, creamy sage risotto, beautifully cooked shallots and a delicious reduction sauce.

Portions at the Hamborough are small so there was plenty of room for my prune trio of hot prune and armanac soufflé, a dollop of marinated prunes and an intense prune ice cream.

Portions were small and on my second visit I am still desperate for some vegetables with my meal yet I left feeling full up. That's rich food for you. *Phone 01983 856333*

The Royal Hotel ★★★

Compared to restaurants, bistros and pubs, dining room eating is a rather genteel affair. Normally raucous parties take on a subdued demeanour, conversations become hushed - one is exposed enough in such a large open expanse of room. Even children assume the behaviour of one intimidated by their surroundings. Dining rooms call for formality, although thank god the silver service has been abandoned. These days what is on the plate is all down to the chef. On the down side veg' portions have disappeared and reappeared as garnish. The dining room at the Royal is large and simply furnished the expanse broken up with a wall partition. Peach coloured walls, dark blue soft furnishings, old gold framed oils, chandeliers, a bust and a slightly out of place art deco mirror complete the look. Service with a smile is discreet but at the same time attentive. I nibbled on a walnut and brown bread roll (H'made) while I waited my first course, a slice of terrine made up of confit of duck, foie gras and pasta, it was served with delicate orange segments and a light dressing. It was very good. I wasn't going to have a second roll when offered, but I was glad I changed my mind as portions are very small. My main course of steamed sea-bream, stuffed with scallop mousse on a small bed of couscous was delicate on all counts, flavour, texture and size. It came with 4 spears of peeled (shows attention to detail) char-grilled asparagus. It was all delicious but I wanted more. The tiny dessert of roasted caramelised pineapple (sweet with a tangy edge) with malibu panna cotta, a tender wobbly creation, it was a delectable but wicked tease. *Phone 01983 852186*

Best of Wight 2006/07

Best Café
Apple Tree Cafe

Best Pub Specials Board
The Crown Inn

Best "Bistro" Style Restaurant
The St Helens Restaurant

Best "State of the Art"
Gourmet Restaurant
The Essex

Best Food Shop
Godshill Organics

Best Ingredient
Blakes Hut, Ventnor, for local crab

Best All-Rounder
The St Helens Restaurant

17

The Boat House Seafood Restaurant *

Imagine the tropics, imagine alfresco eating under the gentle shade of a palm-fringed veranda and you have The Boat House. What pleasure and how clever to think of planting a piece of the South Sea Islands on our own Wighty shores.

Wooden slatted floors, canvas roof, directors chairs, bits of old rope twisted around driftwood rails. Stones off the beach, trellis walls and trees growing through the floor contrast with damask napkins and large glass goblets for the delicious house wine.

The menu is basically salad, salad and salad. I had the seafood platter with an almost perfectly cooked lobster. A crab shell filled with hand-picked succulent brown and white crab meat and a dozen shell on prawns resting on a large bed of salad. The seafood was incredibly fresh. The only thing missing was a dollop of home-made mayonnaise.

Puds were not home-made on the day I visited. You will not have room for one anyway so don't worry about it. I was however, pleased to see that they sold Minghella ice creams.

I dropped in for lunch mid-week at the end of August and was lucky to get a table. In the end they were probably pleased to see me because a prominent Island family had booked and failed to turn up. Service was friendly, helpful and I felt genuinely welcome.

Phone 01983 852747

YARMOUTH

The George Hotel Brasserie ★★

Although it is a brasserie on my second visit the brasserie food was being served in the restaurant, and in a marquee, while the brasserie room was being pulled apart at the seams (refurbishment).

This is in my opinion the most expensive restaurant on the Island particuarly as the definition of brasserie is a small and usually cheap restaurant. It offers an interesting range of dishes often using luxury ingredients such as oysters, foie gras and girolles. My warm starter of confit of artichokes, beetroot, girolles, parmesan shavings and soft boiled egg was acceptable. My main dish was a good combination of sea bass with spider crab, pink grapefruit and lobster foam. The mixed veg' of mange tout, sugar peas, French beans and courgettes were more crunchy then al dente which made eating them hard going and the Jersey Royal potatoes would have been nicer if they had been scrubbed clean. Portions are rich an generous so I went for a light dessert of strawberries in sabayon au gratin. Sabayon is egg yolks whisked to a thick foam with sugar and usually Marsala over a double saucepan. My pudding was in fact strawberries topped with cold egg custard then grilled—it was nice but it wasn't sabayon.

Phone 01983 760331

The Blue Crab **+

I have always had this belief that there are two kinds of good chef. There is the one who takes. That is he produces quality food to clinical perfection in exchange for masses of money. Then there is the giver, the chef who loves to feed and nurture all those hungry bodies with quality, well cooked wholesome food. The chef at the Blue Crab is the latter. He obviously loves to eat and he is not interested in rations and squiggles of sauce garnishing a spotlessly white plate.

The food is rustic, robust and generous. My starter of mussels and bacon were delicious albeit rather rich.The menu is predominantly fish so I opted for the Whole grilled Sea bass with creamy tarragon sauce. I have always moaned about plates that are too small for the food but in this case the plate was actually quite large, but the bass was even larger. I was sure I wouldn't eat it all—I had to save room for the pudding—but it was so fresh, so dripping in butter, so tender and so tasty, probably because it had been cooked on the bone, that I ate the lot. This guy knows how to cook fish.

Pudding selection was again rustic and robust, Pear Crumble, Sticky chocolate pudding etc. I went for the Marmalade Bread and Butter pudding, but in fact it wasn't. There was too much bread and not enough baked custard and it was made with brioche—I decided that I would just give it a taster, I was still full from buttery fish. I don't know where I put it but it was so light and delicious that I again I ate the lot. Service is friendly and rather quaint.
Phone 01983 760014

The Wight Good Food Guide does not like being asked by a credit card machine if it wants to give a tip—particularly after having had a few drinks!

MASTER CLASS

Perfect Cappuccino

Cappuccino coffee is the one drink that I get really annoyed about. Most establishments think that as long as it has chocolate sprinkled on the top, that is all it requires. Then there are those that think it has to have the froth piled on top like a snow capped mountain. A real cappuccino is ⅓ coffee, ⅓ milk and ⅓ froth all below the rim of the cup. Milk to the rim is a Latte. A large cappuccino should never be served in a mug, that is disgusting. The chocolate topping should be cocoa, not sprinkles and this is why I always ask for my cappuccino without the chocolate topping as no one ever seems to use cocoa anymore. Nevertheless, to date Thorntons in Newport is the closest anyone on the Island gets to a good cappuccino.

ISLAND ROUND-UP of more foody recommendations

Pub Special Boards

The New Inn, Shalfleet for their sea-food specials

Crab and Lobster, Bembridge for their crab salads

The White Lion, Arreton for their creamy Fisherman's pie

Cafés and Restaurants

The Old Smithy, Godshill for their delicious cream cakes

Warren Farm, Alum Bay for their ham sandwiches and venue

Waters Edge, Gurnard for their venue and chicken wraps

Beach Café, Steephill Cove, Ventnor for their delicious crab sandwiches and pink meringues

Osborne House Café, East Cowes for their snacks

Devonia Kiosk, Sandown Bay for their soups

The Lavender Farm, Newport for their lavender ice-cream and short-bread

Thorntons, Newport for the best chain, excellent cakes, and coffee

Chessell Pottery, Chessell for their very simple food, very small menu, very fresh flavours.

Brighstone Tearooms, Brighstone for knowing it's limitations. Planning for a busy season it is offering bought in food from local producers, sau-sages with speciality mashes, ice-creams and cakes. Blackboard menu offers simple well presented dishes served with organic vegetables.

Traditional Sunday Lunch

Black Cat, Freshwater Bay

Crown Inn, Shorwell

Royal Hotel, Ventnor

Albert Cottage, East Cowes

Shopping

Blakes on the pier at Ventnor for fantastically fresh fish off the boat

Wheelers at Steephill cove for crab and lobsters

Minghellas ginger ice-cream amongst others

Calbourne Classics ice-cream and tray bakes

Chale Farm for their Christmas ice-cream

Godshill Organics for the best independent farm shop (also totally organic)

Afton Park, Freshwater for rare breeds beef, apple juice and other food specialities

Freshwater Bakery, Freshwater for delicious crusty bread

Mapes Bakery, Sandown for a wide range of dough-nuts

Albert Cottage Restaurant
Proprietor/Manager: Rachel Fiddler
Chef: Steve Shakeshaft
Address: York Avenue, East Cowes
Tel no: 01983 299309
Opening hours: 6.30 pm to 9.00 pm
Last orders: 8.30 pm

Apple Tree Café at Afton Park
Proprietor/Manager: Mr and Mrs Heathcote
Chef: Wendy Newnham & Phil Blair
Address: Afton Park Ltd, Newport Road, AFTON, Nr Freshwater
Tel no: 01983 755774
Opening hours: 9.00 am to 6.00 pm
Last orders: Food 10.00 am to 4.00 pm
Min amount accepted on credit cards: £10

Burrs Restaurant
Proprietor/Manager: Michael Burr
Chef: Michael Burr
Address: 27A Lugley Street, Newport
Tel no: 01983 825470
Opening hours: 7.00 pm to 9.30 pm
Last orders: 9.30 pm

The Blue Crab
Proprietor/Manager: Miss Ruth Gardner and Mr
Cliff McDonald
Chef: Cliff McDonald
Address: High Street, Yarmouth
Tel no: 01983 760014
Opening hours: Winter: Tues to Sun 11.00 am to
3.00 pm and 6.30 pm to 11.00 pm. Summer holi-
days: 7 days 11.00 am to 3.00 pm and 6.30 pm to
11.00 pm
Last orders: 10.00 pm

The Boat House Seafood Restaurant
Proprietor/Manager: Mark and Vanessa Wheeler
Chef: Vanessa Wheeler
Address: Steephill Cove, Ventnor
Tel no: 01983 852747
Opening hours: Lunch 12.30 pm to 1.45 pm
Last orders: 1.45 pm
Credit cards: Not accepted

Bonchurch Inn
Address: Bonchurch Shute, Bonchurch
Tel no: 01983 852611

The Crown Inn
Proprietor/Manager: Sally and Luke Grace
Chef: Kieron Barton
Address: Walkers Lane, Shorwell
Tel no: 01983 740293
Opening hours: 10.30 am to 3.00pm and 6.00 pm
to 10.30 pm—extended in the summer
Min amount accepted on credit cards: £6.00

The Essex
Proprietor/Manager: Kathy and Mark Domaille
Chef: Steve Harris
Address: High Street Godshill
Tel no: 01983 840232
Opening hours: 12.00 midday to 3.30 pm then 6
pm onwards
Last orders: 3.00 pm and 9.30 pm

Fighting Cocks
Proprietor/Manager: Gillian Bell
Chef: Berni Nigh and Paul Mills
Address: Hale Common, Arreton
Tel no: 01983 865254
Opening hours: Mon to Sat 11.00 am to 11.00 pm

(note: winter times may vary)
Min amount accepted on credit cards: £5

Fultons Seafood and Chop House
Proprietor/Manager: Ian and Karen Whitehead
Chef: Mathew Rayment
Address: Sherborne Street, Bembridge
Tel no: 01983 875559
*Food served :*12 midday to 2.30 pm and 6.00 pm
to 10.00 pm.
Last orders: Food 9.45 pm

The George Hotel Restaurant and Bistro
Proprietor/Manager: Jeremy Wilcock
Chef: José Graziosi
Address: Quay Street, Yarmouth
Tel no: 01983 760331
Opening hours: Lunch 12 midday to 3.00 pm.
Dinner 7.00 pm to 10.00 pm
Last orders: Lunch 3.00 pm Evening 10.00 pm

Gods Providence House
Proprietor/Manager: Andy Willard and Lynne
Saunders
Address: 12 St Thomas Square, Newport
Tel no: 01983 522088
Opening hours: Mon to Sat 9.00 am to 5 pm, Sun
10.00 am to 3.00 pm
Min amount accepted on credit cards: £10

The Hambrough Hotel
Proprietor/Manager: Jo dos Santos
Chef: Craig Atchinson
Address: Hamborough Road, Ventnor
Tel no: 01983 856333
Opening hours: Lunch 12 midday to 3.00 pm and
evening 7.00 pm to 9.30 pm. Closed all day Tues-
day and Sun Eve.

Liberties
Proprietor/Manager: Annie Horne
Chef: Kevin Hendy
Address: 12 Union Street, Ryde
Tel no: 811007
Opening hours: Mon to Wed 10 am to 11 pm. Thu
to Sat 10 am to 12 midnight. Sun 11 am to 11 pm
Last orders: 9.30 pm

Mojacs Restaurant
Proprietor/Manager: Mark and Helen Baldwin
Chef: Mark Baldwin
Address: 10A Shooters Hill, Cowes
Tel no: 01983 28118
Opening hours: Lunch—bookings only. Evening
6.30 pm to 9.30
Last orders: 9.30 pm

Morgans Restaurant
Proprietor/Manager: Tim Morgan
Chef: Tim Morgan
Address: 36-38 High Street, Shanklin
Tel no: 01983 864900
Opening hours: 12 midday to 2.00 pm and 7.00 pm to 9.00 pm
Min amount accepted on credit cards: £20

Olivo Restaurant
Chef: Rasta
Address: 15 St Thomas Square, Newport
Tel no: 01983 520002
Opening hours: 9.00 am to 11.00 pm
Last orders: 9.15 pm

The Pond Café
Proprietor/Manager: Jo dos Santos
Chef: Luke Borley
Address: Bonchurch Village Road, Bonchurch
Tel no: 01983 855666
Opening hours: Lunch 10.00 am to 2.00 pm and evening 7.00 pm to 9.00 pm
Last orders: Lunch 2.00 pm Eve 9.00 pm

Priory Bay Hotel
Proprietor/Manager: Andrew Palmer
Chef: Chris Turner
Address: Priory Drive, Seaview
Tel no: 01983 613146
Opening hours: 12.30 pm to 2.00 pm and 7.00 pm to 9.15 pm
Last orders: 9.15 pm

Quay Arts Café
Manager: Jo Cowan
Address: Sea Street, Newport
Tel no: 01983 822490
Opening hours: Mon to Sat 9.30 am to 4.30 pm
Last orders: 3.00 pm for food most days
Min amount accepted on credit cards: £5

The Red Lion
Proprietor: Michael Mence
Chef: Lorna Mence
Address: Church Place, Freshwater
Tel no: 01983 754925
Food served: 12.00 midday to 2.00 pm and 6.30 pm to 9.00 pm (Sun from 7.00 pm)
Last orders: As above
Min amount accepted on credit cards: £10

The Royal Hotel Ltd
Owner: William Bailey *Manager:* Jennie McKee
Chef: Alan Staley
Address: Belgrave Road, Ventnor
Tel no: 01983 852186
Opening hours: 6.45 pm to 9.00 pm
Time of last orders: 9.00 pm

Saffrons
Proprietor: Michael and Emma Paine
Chef: Michael Paine
Address: 29 North Road, Shanklin
Tel no: 01983 861589
Opening hours: Mon to Sat 6.00 pm 'til late

Seaview Hotel Restaurant
Proprietor/manager: Andrew Morgan
Chef: Graham Walker
Address: The High Street, Seaview
Tel no: 01983 612711
Opening hours: 6.30 pm to 9.30 pm

The St Helens Restaurant
Proprietor: Mark Young and Lian Beadell
Chef: Mark Young
Address: Lower Green Road, St Helens, Ryde
Tel no: 01983 872303
Opening hours: Summer 7 nights a week 6.30pm plus Sunday Brunch, Winter 4/5 nights a week 6.30 pm plus Sunday Brunch
Min amount accepted on credit cards: £5

Steephill Cove Beach Café
Proprietor/Manager: Bill and Jayne Nigh
Chef: Bill and Jayne Nigh
Address: Steephill Cove, Ventnor
Tel no: 01983 855390
Opening hours: Mon to Sat 10.30 am to 5.00 pm. Sun 11.00 am to 5.00 pm
Last orders: Food served all day (subject to availability)

The Terrace Restaurant at Osborne House
Proprietor: Heidi Kimber-French
Chef: Ray Heward
Address: Osborne House, East Cowes
Tel no: 01983 298052
Opening hours: Lunch only 12 midday to 3.30
Min amount accepted on credit cards: £5

What's Cooking on the Isle of Wight

*F*irst and foremost I'm a gourmet and a chef, so when I set out to gather together the recipes for this book I was determined that the ones I chose should be enjoyable to eat. Dipping into the past in search of traditional recipes, it immediately struck me that most wouldn't suit today's palate: indeed some recipes such as 'Mackerel Boiled in Brine' would be positively inedible!

In addition, many new ingredients have been introduced to us over the past thirty years or so. Much old-fashioned traditional cooking, with a few honorable exceptions, would now taste bland. Hopefully this book will redress the balance.

If spectacular recipes don't abound, then the marvellous food produced by the Island's micro-climate more than compensates. Isle of Wight Cookery is a celebration of an `Island Retreat' dedicated to self-sufficiency, market gardening, and good wholesome eating—where the quality of food speaks for itself.

The Isle of Wight is small, a mere 94,000 acres of varied soils. The landscape, which includes open down-land, intimate valleys, lush grazing land and broad-leaved forests, is as diverse and rich in natural beauty as anywhere in England. For at least the last two centuries it has been known as the 'Garden of England'. Its greatest blessing is its protected position off the southern coast, which has given it a mild temperate climate. Extremes are rare, and snow seldom settles, even on its highest hills.

The mild winters and extended summers give the Island's farmers and market-gardeners a lengthier growing season than many other parts of the country. We can, for instance, enjoy sweet fresh strawberries from as early as May to as late as November. The arable soils of the Arreton valley in the center of the Island have long been famous for their fertility, as good for barley and sheep as they are for asparagus and strawberries.

There's also no shortage of food to be harvested from the seas around the Island's coast, including sea bass, plaice, mackerel and herring. Shellfish are a particular speciality of the Island, and both crab and lobster lunches are easy to find in many of the pubs, restaurants and cafes. For those with a thirst, there are the wines from Island vineyards, an Island brewed beer, our own bottled water, as well as apple juice and fruit wines and cider.

This sense of self-sufficiency undoubtedly owes its origins to the Island's insularity. Today, many innovative locals have set up splendid businesses based on food, offering first-class `home-made' style produce, from ice-cream to smoked salmon, farm honey, speciality mustards and gourmet sausages.

Some 20 years ago locally produced meat had a crisis when the abattoir was closed down. It became impossible to buy locally produced meat. However, once again meat is now being reared on the Island for island consumption. All of it a superb quality including, lamb, pork, beef and a wide range of poultry including bronze turkey and goose for Christmas.

Perhaps the greatest success has been that of a once uncommon bulb—garlic. Thanks to the Boswell family the Island is now firmly on the international agricultural map. Its pungent aroma seasons the air in Arreton Valley, and every August, at the annual Garlic Festival, over twenty thousand people gather to sample such delights as garlic flavoured ice-cream, lager, mushrooms and prawns.

The growing season on the Island never seems to stop, and as one year of plenty rolls into another, the demand for the Island's produce becomes greater than ever.

Perhaps more importantly, the Island has long been considered a holiday resort and it has been a tradition for our numerous inns and teashops to provide sustenance for its many visitors. In the past many premises had their own baker's ovens and produced a variety of small cakes, particularly the popular `Isle of Wight Doughnut'. The popularity of the afternoon tea has grown, and many establishments offering good home cooking are open throughout the year.

The recipes in this book have been chosen to reflect the splendid and prolific raw materials available to Islanders and the Island's many chefs. Because of the quality of produce simple recipes have proven to be best, and traditional recipes have been rewritten with modern tastes in mind.

A lot of the recipes in this section were served at my restaurant Lugley's, Newport which later moved out to Wootton.

Layered Crab Mousse

This recipe is enhanced if served with a lightly flavoured curry mayonnaise.

8 oz (225gm) brown crab meat
8 oz (225gm) white crab meat
4 tbls mayonnaise
small tub double cream
1 tbls tomato ketchup
2 tbls lemon juice
several dashes Tabasco sauce according to taste
1 lb (450gm) large spinach leaves
salt and freshly ground black pepper
1 sachet of gelatine crystals

To the brown crab meat add 2 tbsp of mayonnaise and the tomato ketchup, and mix thoroughly. To the white crab meat add the remaining 2 tbsp of mayonnaise and the Tabasco sauce and mix thoroughly. Season both meats with salt and black pepper.

Blanch the spinach leaves in boiling water just long enough to wilt them. Then plunge into cold water to arrest the process. Line a one pint (570 ml) terrine dish with the spinach leaves, with enough hanging over the sides to fold back over the top.

Soften the gelatine crystals in the lemon juice with an extra tbsp of cold water, then heat gently in a double saucepan to melt the crystals.

Whip the cream until it is fairly stiff.

Working quickly, mix half of the melted gelatine into the brown crab mixture then fold in half the whipped cream. Pour into the bottom of the mould. Pop in the freezer for ten minutes to firm up quickly.

Mix the remaining melted gelatine with the white crab meat and fold in the rest of the whipped cream. Take the terrine out of the freezer and very carefully layer the white crab meat on top of the brown. Fold over the spinach leaves and put to chill in the refrigerator for 4 hours or overnight.

To serve, turn out of the terrine and cut into wedges. Pour a little curry mayonnaise around the edge and serve with toasted pitta bread. Serves 4-6.

Baked Egg and Smoked Haddock en Cocotte

This simple and delicious dish using the best dairy produce was one of Lugley's signature dishes.

4 medium eggs
8 oz (225gm) smoked haddock, diced
1 finely chopped onion, softened in butter
8 tbls double cream, (approx) must be double
4 oz (II0gm) mature cheddar cheese, (be generous)
salt and pepper

Pre-heat oven to its highest setting.

Divide the onion between four large cocotte dishes. Arrange the diced haddock around the edge of the dish, leaving a hollow in the centre. Break 1 egg in the centre of each hollow, then pour over the cream about 2tbls per cocotte.Grate the cheddar and sprinkle generous amounts on top.

Place the cocottes on a baking tray and put in the oven for 15-20 minutes depending how well you like your eggs done. Garnish with a sprig of fresh herbs.

Variations - smoked ham, cooked leeks, sauced mushrooms, cooked spinach, chopped tomatoes, prawns, left over bolognaise./ Stilton che(goats milk cheese, roqueforte cheese, emmental and gruyer cheese.

Sauté of Chicken Livers with Brandy and Cream

The sauce from the chicken livers acts as a delicious dressing for the salad leaves.

1lb (450gm) chicken livers
4 rashers smoked streaky bacon
1 medium onion finely chopped
1 tbls wholegrain mustard
2 tbls oil and tbls softened butter
generous tot of inexpensive brandy
2 tbls whipped cream
selection of crisp salad leaves

Arrange the salad leaves on four individual plates, ready to take the chicken livers.

Gently heat the oil and butter in a frying pan. Cut the bacon into small lardons and add to the pan. Sauté for a couple of minutes then add the finely chopped onion. Cook until the onion is golden.

Slice the chicken livers into strips. Raise the heat under the pan slightly and add the chicken livers. Turn them in the pan constantly for no more than 2 minutes. Add salt, freshly-ground black pepper and the brandy. Flame while the sauce is bubbling, then quickly swirl in the whipped cream. Turn out of the pan onto the salad leaves and serve with crusty French bread. Serves 4.

Sophisticated Kedgeree

In the time of the Victorian Empire kedgeree was a breakfast dish.

8 quail eggs
8 oz (225gm) smoked haddock,
2 this finely chopped onion, softened in butter
I teaspoon or more (depending upon to taste) of curry paste
small pot double cream
4 oz (110gm) basmati rice gently cooked so that the grains do not stick together
milk to cover the smoked haddock
freshly chopped parsley

Poach the haddock in the milk in a frying pan over a gentle heat on top of the stove until just cooked—the flakes should still be creamy.

Meanwhile gently cook the basmati rice—do not boil as this will fracture the grains and make the rice sticky.

Place the quail eggs in a pan of cold water. Slowly bring to the boil then remove from the heat and stand for 4 minutes. Then put into cold water to arrest the cooking process.

Keep the haddock and the rice warm.

In a small saucepan mix the cream with the curry paste and some of the milk stock from the smoked haddock. Bring to the boil and then simmer until thick.

Press the rice into 4 lightly oiled moulds then turn out onto warm serving plates (or pile rustically in the centre of the plates. Arrange large flakes of smoked haddock around the rice. Drizzle the curry sauce over the dish and garnish with the lightly boiled shelled and halved quails eggs. Garnish with chopped parsley.

Local Seafood

*T*he waters surrounding the Isle of Wight provide the local residents and holiday-makers with an abundant and varied choice of fish, and fresh fish meals can be found on many of the Island's restaurant and pub menus. At lunch times, local crab sandwiches on wholemeal bread or tasty crab salads are a popular choice; and a must for Island visitors.

Surprisingly, in restaurants the two most popular seafood's are in fact the most luxurious. Lobster, which is a supreme delicacy and sea bass, which was elevated onto a pedestal in the eighties and has a fine meaty texture and taste. But this is just two of a marvelous selection caught in the waters surrounding the Island.

Plaice is very popular with the locals, it seems to be plumper than anywhere else, as is the local lemon sole, brill, turbot and the smaller dabs.

Cod is no longer the cheap food it used to be, which in a way is a good thing, because it can now be enjoyed for its large meaty, creamy flakes and flavour rather than for its economical price. As with sea bass it is quite common to see a large gleaming 25lb cod lying next to a group of small 1lb codlings, giving you a choice of one fish per person or chunky, white cod steaks. Freshly caught haddock is also worth looking out for.

Amongst the oily fish there is always a choice of fresh mackerel, herrings, sprats and grey mullet, their abundance varying upon their seasonal availability.

If you are up early enough, you can buy your fish from the local fisherman as he brings in his night's catch. However, what isn't sold from the beach finds its way to the local fishmongers. The best on the Island are Blakes on the Pier, Ventnor: Phillip's Fine Foods just outside Cowes and Captain Stan, Bembridge.

Sea Bass with Saffron and Scallops

Sea Bass

Sea bass is one of England's greatest glories, with a price to match. But if nothing else it is plentiful around the Isle of Wight and its freshness is guaranteed. Bass has a delicious, moist, firm, meaty flesh and a pretty delicate silvery skin that I always leave intact. Having become—because of the price—such a special occasion fish, the next three recipes are intended to reflect that fact. (Farmed sea-bass is much cheaper.)

2 sea bass — each about 1 lb (450gm) in weight
8 fresh scallops,
½ pt (275ml) dry white wine
½ pt (275ml) fish stock made from the bones
1 small sachet of saffron strands or powder
1 large onion,
1 clove of garlic
4 tbsp double cream or 4 tbsp milk mixed with
2 tspn cornflour, salt and pepper

Remove the large scales and the head from the fish and then fillet. Be careful how you do this as sea bass bones are very spiky and can give you a nasty stab. (If in doubt ask your fishmonger to do it for you but make sure he gives you the bones and head for the stock.)

Lay the fish in a shallow roasting pan surrounded with a scant ½ inch of water or white wine. Cover with tin foil to seal in the steam and bake in a hot oven preheated to 425°F/220°C/Gas Mark 7 for 20 minutes. Be careful not to overcook the fish. Test at the 15 minutes stage with a skewer. If it slides through the fish easily then it is done.

Meanwhile make the sauce. You may want to start this before you put the fish in to cook. In a saucepan put the white wine, fish stock, saffron, garlic, and the onion which has been skinned, and cut into quarters. Simmer gently until the stock has reduced by half and the onion is soft and pulpy. Add the cream or the cornflour blended with the milk and, in the latter case, stirring all the time, simmer for a further 15 minutes. When thickened, put in a blender, whiz until smooth and then pass through a sieve. Return to the saucepan. Season to taste (at this stage the sea bass can be put in the oven to cook).

Roughly chop the scallops, and 2 minutes before serving the dish pop the scallops into the simmering sauce. This is just long enough to cook them without overcooking. Arrange the sea bass fillets on individual plates and surround with the delicious sauce. Serves 4.

Herrings in Oatmeal with Gooseberry Sauce

4 large fresh herrings
4 tbls medium oatmeal
salt and pepper
olive oil for frying
8 oz (225gm) gooseberries
4 oz (110gm) castor sugar
(use less sugar for a sharper
taste)
1 oz (25gm) fresh chopped
mint
2 oz (50gm) butter

Thoroughly clean then fillet the herrings. Season with salt and pepper, then coat in the oatmeal pressing the oats to the damp flesh. Put to one side while you make the sauce.

Top and tail the gooseberries and put in an enamel or stainless steel saucepan with the chopped mint, castor sugar and the butter. Cover with a lid and stew very gently over a low heat for 30 minutes until a sauce has formed. Keep warm.

Heat the oil in a large frying pan and when hot sâuté the herring fillets about 4 minutes each side or until the oatmeal turns a delicious crunchy golden brown. Serve immediately with the warm gooseberry sauce and a crisp green side salad.

NB Traditionally this sauce is served with mackerel, so keep an open mind when shopping and buy whichever fish is freshest. Serves 4.

Three courses from the kitchen of The Blue Crab

Potted Crayfish Tails

4 oz (110gm) butter
8 oz (225gm) crayfish tails
¼ of onion finely diced
pinch blade mace or ¼ teaspoon powdered
¼ teaspoon nutmeg
pinch sea salt
3 or 4 good grinds of black pepper
2 tablespoons of chopped parsley
squeeze of lemon juice
clarified butter

First melt the butter in a thick-bottomed pan over a moderate heat, then add the onions and cook until soft and opaque. Stir in the crayfish, mace, nutmeg, sea salt, pepper and heat thoroughly. Be careful not to let them boil as it toughens the crayfish tails. Stir them as they cook. Take off the heat and stir in a squeeze of lemon juice and the chopped parsley.

Divide into 4 ramekins. Seal with the clarified butter. Leave in the fridge until chilled. Serve with warm crusty or granary bread.
Serves 4.

Smoked Haddock Rarebit with Red Onion and Tomato Salad

smoked haddock about 8-12 oz (225-250gm)

for the rarebit mix
8 oz (225gm) of grated cheese
pinch of cayenne pepper
couple of good grinds of the pepper mill
1 x egg
5 oz (150ml) good beer
1 teaspoon English mustard

2 large beef tomatoes Sliced
½ red onion sliced
mixed salad leaves

Pre heat oven to 180°C
First mix all the ingredients for the rarebit and place in the fridge. Bake the smoked haddock until half cooked then place the rarebit mixture on top of the haddock and bake until golden brown. While the haddock is baking, fan the tomatoes in a ring on a plate and stack the leaves in the center. Scatter the onions over the top of the leaves and drizzle with olive oil. To finish, place the haddock on the top and serve.
Serves 4.

Crème Caramel with Star Anise

3½ oz (100gm) sugar
4 fl oz (125ml) water
scant 1pt (½ ltr) milk
4 eggs
2 oz (50gm) sugar
seeds from a vanilla pod
2 star anise

First warm the milk with the vanilla seeds and 2 star anise and leave to infuse.

Make the caramel by boiling ¾ of the water with the 3½ oz (100gm) of sugar in a thick-bottomed pan until golden brown. When cooked add the remainder of the water and re-boil until the sugar and water mix, be careful when adding the water it does spit a bit. Pour into 6 Dariole moulds or ramekins. Whisk the milk onto the eggs and sugar. Strain and pour into the moulds. Place into a deep tray and half fill with water. Cook in a moderate oven (150°C-160°C) for about 30 mins or until set. When cold loosen around the edges with fingers and shake firmly to loosen. Turn out into a flat plate or dish. Pour any remaining caramel into the moulds around the crèmes and serve.
Serves 6.

The Value of Meat

*M*ore than anything it is important to eat a balanced diet, yet because of
the bad, sometimes uninformed publicity over recent years, more people have ceased to eat meat—therefore, unbalancing their diet.

Meat is extremely good for you and meat products in general, such as milk
and eggs, are essential for a healthy diet. If you cut them out, as vegans do,
then artificial substitutes have to be taken to replace lost nutriments.

Looking at it scientifically, the body needs the building blocks of protein
which are amino acids. The body is unable to manufacture these acids so it
has to get them from 'high-quality' protein which is found in meat. Protein is
essential to everyone but particularly to children who have fast growing bodies. The body also needs vitamin B12 and meat products are virtually the
only dietary source: plant foods lack vitamin B12.

Minerals are also important. Iron, it's true, is available in grains, nuts and
pulses (via baked products) but by far the best source is meat, simply because it is chemically bound to the blood protein hemoglobin and is, therefore, rapidly absorbed into the blood. This is not the case with iron found in
plants and lack of iron can cause anemia.

The amount of meat required for a healthy diet depends on whether you
are male or female, a pregnant woman or a growing child (both by the way
need the most). The average person within these categories requires 6-9 oz
of meat (or fish) per day. We are not talking 16 oz T Bone steaks here but a
few slices of roast beef or an average sized chicken breast.

Unbeknown to many people, most meat is reared in happy conditions.
Fields full of cows (beef) and sheep (lamb) is proof of that, and in fact have
always been reared that way; and these days it is not uncommon to see pigs
rooting around in open fields. Battery chickens do still sadly exist but are
very cheap. For a little extra money you can easily purchase a free range
chicken. The more of you that do so the more common, and eventually
cheaper, free range chickens (and eggs) will become.

It is not in the farmer's interest to neglect his animals unless he wants to
fork out money for hefty vet's bills; and an animal that has been stressed in
the slaughterhouse, as so many people claim, results in inedible meat.
What's the point of that!

In the same way that a damaged apple is inedible so is damaged meat,
and great care is taken that this should not happen. At least the meat you
eat has not been sprayed with insecticide and if an animal is ill, the antibiot-
ics it is given to help its recovery are no more harmful than the ones the doctor gives us to aid our own recovery.

Meat is essential for the development of strong healthy children and very
important to people in active work, be it for pleasure or pay.

The Noble Asparagus

*T*his princely vegetable possesses a regality difficult for any other vegetable to compete with. Rarely is it served as an accompanying vegetable. It is much too special for that.

You need to be a patient gardener to grow this elegant vegetable. It takes four years for an asparagus bed to grow strong and develop into a prosperous plant. But the reward is fresh asparagus for as much as twenty years.

The Island's light, fertile soil is well suited to asparagus growing, and because it is a cool weather crop it provides us with an early taste of summer.

To ensure a strong plant, the first year's harvest of spindly spears should be left untouched. The second year a few stems can be gathered and a few more the third year. The first real harvest is on the fourth year and every year after that providing you treat your asparagus bed kindly.

So cherished is this vegetable, an industry of specially designed pots has emerged in which to cook these precious spears. Designed to cook the stems in boiling water while at the same time cooking the tender tips in the hotter than boiling steam trapped at the top of the pot, results in the tips becoming over-cooked; which seems to render the pots ineffective! The best method is to fill a pan, wide enough to take the stems lying down, with water. Bring to the boil, drop in the spears then rapidly simmer in the water for 6-8 minutes depending on the thickness of the stems. Remove with a fish slice and drain on a cake rack.

To prepare before cooking, cut off the woody base. This is done by trial and error, but you'll soon get the hang of it. If you are a perfectionist, remove the thin, stringy skin on the stems with a potato peeler.

Asparagus is best when bought the same day it is picked. After that the sterns progressively lose their crispness and begin to shrivel. Some of the freshest asparagus on the Island can be bought at the Garlic Farm Shop, Newchurch, from April to June.

Asparagus Soup with Courgette Mousse

1lb (450gm) grade 2 asparagus
1 small finely chopped onion
1 small clove garlic
2 tbls oil and 2 tbls softened butter
1pt (575ml) chicken or vegetable stock
salt and pepper
4 tbls single cream
1lb (450gm) small, firm courgettes
2 tbls oil
2 tbls freshly chopped tarragon
4 size 2 eggs
⅓ pt (250ml) 1 double cream
salt and pepper
softened butter

Remove the spears from the tops of the asparagus and reserve. With a potato peeler remove the stringy outer skins from the stems and cut into 1 inch (2.5cm) pieces (discard the woody bits). Heat the oil and half the butter in a large saucepan and add the onion, garlic and stems. Sweat slowly for 15 minutes. Add the stock and simmer for a further 15 minutes.

Purée the soup and pass through a sieve. Return to the saucepan and add the rest of the butter, the cream, seasoning and asparagus tips then simmer until the tips are tender.

To make the mousses: slice the courgettes and soften gently in the oil in a saucepan. Blend in a processor with the tarragon, eggs, double cream and seasoning.

Liberally butter 6 dariole moulds or cocotte dishes, then spoon in the courgette mixture to the top. Put moulds in a roasting tin half-filled with cold water. Cover with greaseproof paper and cook in the oven Gas Mark 4/180°C/350°F for 30-40 mins or until set. To serve: run a knife around the edges of the mousses and turn out onto soup plates. Surround with the hot asparagus soup and serve immediately. Serves 6.

Feuilette of Asparagus with Mint Béarnaise Sauce

8 oz (225gm) puff pastry
1 lb (450gm) asparagus,
1 shallot
¼ pt (150ml) white wine,
2 tbls white wine vinegar
1 tbls fresh chopped mint,
2 large egg yolks
4 oz (110gm) best butter cut into
cubes

Roll the puff pastry into a rectangle 8 ins ((20cm) long and 4 ins (10cm) wide. Then cut across the width into 4 oblongs. Place on a baking tray. Coat with egg wash and score a pattern on the surface with a fork. Bake in a hot oven 425°F/220°C/Gas Mark 7 for 10 minutes, or until golden in colour. Remove from the oven and cool until ready to use.

Remove the woody bases from the asparagus and with a potato peeler remove the stringy outer skin. Fill a pan, large enough to take the asparagus lying down, with water. Add the asparagus, bring to the boil and simmer for 5 minutes until tender but not too soft. The spears should remain firm and not become floppy.

Meanwhile make the sauce. Place a basin over a saucepan of boiling water. In the basin put the shallot, the wine and the vinegar, heat through. Add the egg yolks and whisk until thick and foamy, and gently heated through. Add the chopped mint then slowly beat in the cubed butter until all used up and a rich sauce has formed. If the sauce is too thick add a tiny drop of wine. **NB** It is essential that you don't overheat the sauce or it will separate.

To serve, heat the puff pastry oblongs through, split open and arrange the drained asparagus on the bottom half. Pour over the minty Béarnaise, and arrange the remaining piece of pastry on the top. Garnish with a fresh sprig of mint. Serves 4.

Leg of Spring Lamb with Creamy Lemon and Mint Sauce

I first served this dish in Lugley's my tiny back-street restaurant over fourteen years ago. It has always been a tremendous success and I have resurrected it many times since.

1 leg of lamb approximately 3 lb (1.4 kg) in weight
1 lemon, cut into thin slices
1 tbsp runny honey
oil, 2 oz (50gm) butter
1 level tbsp plain flour
½ pt (275ml) chicken stock
the juice and grated rind of 1 lemon
1 small tub of soured cream
2 tbsp chopped fresh mint, salt and pepper

Put the leg of lamb in a roasting pan. Arrange the lemon slices on top and dribble over the runny honey. Roast in the oven at Gas Mark 6/400°F/200°C for approximately 1 hour 15 minutes, longer if you like your lamb well done. To test pierce the joint with a skewer, the juice that exudes from the hole should run clear.

Meanwhile make the sauce. Put the butter in a saucepan and add the flour. Cook for a couple of minutes without browning. Stirring all the time add the stock, lemon juice and lemon rind. Cook until thickened then lower the heat and gently simmer for 15 minutes to extract the flavour from the lemon rind.

Remove the lamb from the oven and put to one side to rest. Tip the pan juices into the sauce then add the chopped mint and the soured cream. Simmer for 5 minutes. Carve the meat and serve with the sauce. Accompany with broad beans and sâuté of new potatoes. Serves 4.

Isle of Wight Lamb

*A*s early as the 14th century the Island was a major producer of lamb. Production reached its zenith in the late 18th century when turnips were first grown, thus producing winter fodder. As many as 40,000 sheep were shorn for wool export each year and by the 1800s as many as 1,000 sheep per week were being sent to mainland markets.

It wasn't until much later that dairy cattle were kept on the Island. Before that most of the milk and cheese came from sheep milk. In the late 18th century a cheese called 'Isle of Wight Rock' was produced—though it was considered unpalatable and supposedly required a sledgehammer to cut it. (It sounds similar to parmesan cheese)

From April to September I only ever cook young lamb that needs a short burst of heat under the grill, over a barbecue or in a frying pan. From October to March lamb or better known as hogget tends to be less tender and requires longer, slower cooking.

Lamb Cutlets with Orange and Laverbread Sauce

Laverbread is a puréed seaweed and gives a faintly fishy taste to this dish.

8 Isle of Wight lamb cutlets, oil
1 large onion, skinned and quartered
juice and finely grated rind of 1 orange
1 level tbsp cornflour
1 pt (570 ml) strong, preferably gelatinous, chicken or lamb stock
1 tbsp tinned or frozen laverbread
2 tbsp double cream
salt and lots of black pepper

First prepare the sauce. Put the orange rind, orange juice, onion and stock in a saucepan. Simmer until the onion is soft and the stock is reduced by half. Put into a blender and whiz until smooth. Return to the saucepan and add the laverbread and double cream. Mix the cornflour with a drop of water and add to the sauce. Stirring all the time bring to the boil. Season with salt and pepper.

Smear the lamb cutlets with oil and grill or pan fry for 5 minutes each side. Serve with the sauce, garnished with a thin slice of orange and a sprig of watercress. Accompany with French beans and new potatoes. Serves 4.

Strawberry and Elderflower Sorbet

A perfect sweet to mark the beginning of the season of summer fruits. Throughout June the hedgerows are heavy with fragrant elderflower blossoms. Gather the flowers when the umbels are just beginning to bloom and the blossom is creamy white.

1 lb (450gm) ripe strawberries
8 oz (225gm) castor sugar
½ pt (275ml) water
4 sprays of elderflowers
juice of half a lemon
1 egg white

Put the sugar, water and elderflowers in a saucepan. Heat gently until the sugar has dissolved, then raise the heat and boil the sugar syrup for 15 minutes.

Add the strawberries and lemon juice to the syrup and boil for a further 5 minutes. Remove the elderflowers. Purée the fruit and syrup then push through a fine sieve to remove the strawberry pips. Cool, then pour into a plastic container and freeze to a firmish slush (this will take about 2 hours).

Whisk the egg white in a clean bowl. Then working very quickly, take the sorbet from the freezer, break up with a fork and add to the egg white. Whisk vigorously for 30 seconds until the sorbet has become light and fluffy. It is essential that you work quickly so that it doesn't melt. Quickly spoon back into its plastic container (its bulk will have increased so you may find you need a larger one) and fast freeze for 1 hour. Leave in the freezer until ready to serve. Because of the egg white you should be able to serve this sorbet straight from the freezer. Serves 4—possibly more.

Gooseberry Fool

There are several ways to make fruit fools. Some recipes suggest a mix of stewed fruit and custard, others half custard, half cream and stewed fruit (my own preferred method), whilst others call for all cream and stewed fruit. This recipe uses the latter.

8 oz (225gm) gooseberries
4 oz (110gm) castor sugar, more if the gooseberries are tart
½ pt (275ml) double cream

Top and tail the gooseberries. Put in a pan with the castor sugar, tightly seal with a lid and stew 10-15 minutes or until the fruit is soft and pulpy. Mash the fruit, or purée it for a smooth dessert. Chill.

Whip the cream, fold in the chilled fruit. To serve, pile into glasses and accompany with nutty shortbread biscuits. Serves 4.

Summer Eating

*T*he Isle of Wight offers a spectacular feast. We really come into our own with freshly caught seafood, sea bass, mackerel, crab and lobster. Then of course we have our famous but ephemeral Bermbridge prawns. We have locally grown asparagus, tomatoes and garlic. Juicy soft fruits including delicious strawberries. Wonderful wild flavour enhancers such as elderflowers and seaweed and, now that we have our very own lavender farm thoughts go to lavender flavoured dishes, both sweet and savoury. We are lucky on the Island with our warm weather and compared to the rest of the country the summer season seems to go on and on and on. Because summer on the Island is a longer season than many other parts of the country—although I know some would disagree—this is a longer chapter than the other three.

Lobster Pots

"Plunge into boiling water for 5-10 minutes, remove with a slotted spoon. Crack its shell, season with salt and pepper and serve if wished with brown bread and butter."

No! These aren't instructions on how to boil an egg, but on how to cook a lobster! And it really is as simple as that.

Queen to the court of crustaceans, lobster is very special indeed. A hardy creature with the unusual ability to regenerate lost limbs.

Lobsters are caught during the warm summer months, when sweeter flavoured, by the Island's many dedicated fishermen, in specially hand-woven pots. The pots are designed in such a way that they allow the lobsters in under the temptation of bait but at the same time impede their escape.

The best lobsters are the small one pounders which have a delicate more tender meat. It takes some six years of growing and annually shedding of their shells before they reach this size, about 85 mm in length which is in fact the legal EEC minimum length. Smaller than this and they have to be returned to the sea for another year. It has been known for lobsters to live up to forty years and can weigh in at over thirty-five pounds.

Lobster is nearly always sold cooked, but live is best. They are vicious little beasts and should be handled with care. Although their claws are usually tied up with elastic bands, their tails have the ability to give a nasty pinch, so always handle from above.

To cook a lobster humanely, the RSPCA recommend that it should be laid in a bowl of iced slurry for 20 minutes or in the deep freeze for half an hour. These ice-cold conditions stun the lobster without causing it any distress. It can then be boiled in the normal manner.

Lobster is without doubt a luxury. From a one-pound lobster you will be lucky to extract 7 oz (200gm) of meat and most recipes seem to concentrate on making the most out of a little. Most recipes also call for lobster to be reheated, it is therefore important not to over-cook it in the first place—8 minutes per pound is more than enough.

Lobster Jelly

Every time I make this dish I think of heaven; for this must surely be the sort of food they serve there.

one 2 lb (900gm) live lobster
½ pt (275ml) white wine
1 celery stick, washed
1 carrot, washed
1 leek, washed
3 or 4 fennel seeds
dill or fennel leaves for garnish
1 tbsp lemon juice
½ sachet or 4 leaves of gelatine to set ½ pt (275ml) liquid
6 tbls whipped double cream
1 tbls mayonnaise
¼ peeled and finely diced cucumber

Boil the lobster in 2 pints (1.1ltrs) water for 12 minutes, then shell. Reserve water and shells. To the shell-water, add the vegetables, white wine, shells and fennel seeds. Simmer for about half an hour until the liquid is reduced to about ½ pt (275ml). Strain to remove vegetables etc. Dissolve the gelatine crystals in 2 tbsp cold water, or soften the leaf gelatine in cold water and add to the hot stock with the lemon juice. Slice the tail meat into medallions, and chop the claw and leg meat. Divide this meat between four moulds, reserving the meat from one of the legs and claws. Pour the jellied stock into the moulds to cover the meat then refrigerate until set. If wished, a sprig of fennel or dill can be set in the jelly with the lobster meat.

Finely chop the reserved lobster meat and mix with the mayonnaise, whipped cream and cucumber. Season.

To serve, turn out the jellied lobster and garnish with the fennel or dill leaves and a scoop of lobster cream. Serves 4.

Aromatic Buttered Lobster

The lobster fishing industry is important to the Island and, because they are cheaper here I strongly recommend that you take advantage of them while on the Island—especially during July and August.

4 live lobsters
8 oz (225gm) butter
½ pt (275ml) white wine
¼ tspn ground mace
¼ tspn freshly ground black pepper
4 tbsp freshly chopped, mixed tender herbs i.e. sorrel, dill, tarragon, coriander, mint and parsley, at least 4 types
4 thin slices fresh lemon

Boil the lobsters for 8 minutes in plenty of water. Cool. Remove the shells by splitting in half length ways. Keep one half of each shell to serve as a container for the finished dish.

Melt the butter in a large pan. Add the wine, lemon and spices. Simmer for 4-5 minutes to form a rich sauce. Now add the herbs and seasoning and heat for 1 minute. Add the lobster meat, heat through for a further 2 or 3 minutes. Do not allow to boil or overheat. If the sauce becomes oily add a drop more wine or water to emulsify. Serve this delicious ambrosia in lobster shells with home-made pasta ribbons. Serves 4.

Broad Bean Purée with Fennel

Beans were a staple crop on the Island in the 1790s when arable farming was at its height. Even today the heavy chalk soil on parts of the Island seems to particularly suit broad beans.

Although at their best when picked young, this recipe is perfect for using up large overgrown beans.

2 lb (900gm) broad beans
1 tbsp lemon juice
1 tbsp fennel seeds
salt and pepper
2 oz (50gm) butter or 4 tbsp olive oil
2 tbsp cream

Shell the beans then cook them with the fennel seeds in a pan of boiling water for 15-20 minutes or until tender. Strain through a fine sieve in order to retain the fennel seeds. Put the beans in a blender with the lemon juice, salt and pepper, butter and cream. Whiz to a purée. Serve piping hot with fish, chicken or lamb. Serves 4.

Mussels and Bacon in Garlic and Parsley Butter

Mussels used to be readily available all year round when we had the Oyster Fisheries at Newtown. In fact they are still readily available at supermarket fish counters. Serve with masses of crusty bread to mop up the delicious buttery juices. I often serve in an upturned brioche, split open, so that the mussels appear to be tumbling out of a shell.

2 1b (1 kilo) fresh mussels
1 lb (450gm) smoked streaky bacon
4 cloves garlic
4 oz (110gm) butter
½ oz (10gm) fresh chopped parsley
juice of half a lemon
4 tbsp white wine

Thoroughly scrub the mussels and remove the wiry black beards. Put them in a large heavy-bottomed saucepan and tightly seal with the lid. Place over a high heat for 3 minutes. Remove lid and take out any of the shells that have opened— as you are doing this more shells will begin to open. Continue until all the opened shells are out of the saucepan. Discard any that have refused to open. Remove the mussels from the shells and cool. De-rind the bacon and cut each rasher in half. Wrap around the mussels. If the mussels are small use 2 per piece of bacon.

Mix together the butter, chopped parsley and crushed garlic cloves. Put the mussels and bacon in a deepish grill pan. Dot with half the garlic butter. Place under a hot grill and cook until the bacon is turning a crispy golden colour. (This dish can also be oven baked for 10-15 minutes on high.)

Transfer to the hob. Add the remaining butter, the lemon juice and white wine. Raise the heat and shake the pan around until the liquid has reduced, and an homogenized sauce has developed. Serve rustic type bowls. Serves 4.

Isle of Wight Garlic Festival

*T*he Garlic festival first took hold of the Island in 1984 when the Boswell family, growers of this aromatic bulb, came up with the idea of celebrating the end of the garlic harvest after seeing something similar in the US.

Since then the gate numbers have swollen to such a degree it has now become a two-day event. Over twenty thousand men, women and children, locals and tourists, come together to discover the garlic culture, or cure, as herbalists will tell you.

As you drive through the fertile Arreton Valley it's impossible to miss the garlic-seasoned atmosphere weaving its way through the sun-warmed air. By the time you reach the festival, there is little doubt what is on the menu.

Poor old Dracula, who reviled garlic, would turn in his legendary grave if he could see so many warm-blooded people passionately consuming an amazing garlic ice cream and a remarkable frothy garlic lager, as well as the more traditional garlic-flavoured mushrooms, prawns and bread. It has almost become a foody festival.

Smoked garlic, a more recent and inspired "Boswellian" product has a slightly more subtle taste. Perfect for the garlic waverers. The irony is that some of the Island's garlic ends up in garlic loving France!

There's more than food and live music at the festival. All day long there are special events in the main arena from parachutists to dog display teams. The craft tent shows off the locals' artistic talents. Stalls and sideshows surround the main arena and roving acts, such as the popular Keystone Kops, add a magical spirit to the whole event.

Held every August (the nearest Sunday to the 16th), this is a festival that must not be missed.

Garlic in Red Wine Jelly

A real test for true garlic addicts. Delicious served with crisp salad leaves dressed in good quality olive oil and Salsa Verdi. Also good with thick slices of home-baked ham.

1 sachet aspic crystals
12 oz (350gm) plump garlic cloves
1 large red pepper, finely diced
1 oz (25gm) fresh chopped parsley
olive oil,
¼ pt (150ml) red wine
1 tbls red wine vinegar

Remove the papery skins from the cloves. Put the cloves in a saucepan of cold water and bring to the boil. Drain. Cover with fresh cold water and repeat. Do this 3 times in total. The last time continue simmering until the cloves are tender. Soften the diced pepper in the olive oil.

In a 1 pint (570 ml) terrine, layer the garlic, the pepper and the parsley until all used up. Make up the aspic crystals according to the instructions but substituting a ¼ pt (150 ml) of water with the red wine. Add the vinegar. Pour into the terrine and refrigerate until set.

To serve: cut into thick wedges and garnish with the Salsa Verdi. Serves 4.

Salsa Verdi

There are several versions of this fresh relish. This is the traditional version

1 oz (25gm) fresh parsley
3 or 4 cloves of garlic
1 tbsp capers
1 small tin anchovies
¼ pt (150ml) olive oil

Briefly rinse the anchovies under cold water. Put in a blender with the rest of the ingredients. Whiz until smooth.

Serve with garlic and red wine jelly, pasta, grilled fish and meat dishes.

Cheese and Garlic Herb Pâté

One 8 oz (225gm) tub of cottage cheese
1 small tub of cream cheese
3-4 cloves of garlic
4 tbsp fresh, chopped, mixed herbs
4 spring onions, chopped, including the green part
salt and lots of freshly ground black pepper

Place all the ingredients in a blender or liquidiser and process until smooth. Chill before serving to firm-up the pâté. Serve with toast, celery or apple slices.

Serves 4-6.

Three courses from the kitchen of The St Helens Restaurant

The St Helens Restaurant Basic Bread Recipe

Chef Mark Young says "I have used this recipe with Matt's Wight strong bread flour, Vectis Malty, Wight Spelt, and Wholemeal Spelt, and it works equally well with them all."

2lb 4oz (1kg) Stoneground Flour Company flour
1oz (28gms) dried easyblend yeast
2 tsp salt
1 pt (600ml) hand hot water
1 oz (28gms) Mary Case honey

In one bowl combine water, yeast and honey and leave in a warm place until foaming.

In another bowl combine chosen flour, make a well in the centre and slowly add water and honey mixture, mixing with your hand, until the mixture comes together to form sticky dough.

Turn out onto a floured work surface and knead for 10 mins until smooth and elastic. If the dough is too wet, add more flour until right consistency is achieved. If the dough is too dry, moisten hands with water and knead into the dough until right consistency is achieved. Different flours will incorporate the liquid differently so you may need to adjust the flour and water content as above.

Put the dough into a clean bowl and cover with a tea towel. Leave in a warm place to double in size. Preheat oven to 190°C/375F/Gas Mark 5.

Knock back dough and knead again for a further five mins. You should now have a smooth, elastic dough. Divide between two, 2lb loaf tins. Leave in a warm place until doubled in size, 30 to 40 mins.

Place in centre of preheated oven for 15-20 mins until golden brown on top and base sounds hollow when tapped.

Try to wait at least 10-15 mins before cutting a thick slice and slathering it with Queen Bower butter!

You can use the dough to make any shapes you want but you will need to adjust cooking time and proving times accordingly.

Park Water Farm Herb-crusted Lamb Chops

8 loin chops or 4 Barnsley chops
sprig of rosemary
1 clove of garlic
small handful flat leaf parsley
2 sprigs fresh mint
sea salt and freshly ground pepper
grated zest of a lemon
4 oz (100gm) wholemeal bread
2 tbls Dijon mustard

Preheat oven to 180°C/350F/gas4

To make the herb crust, place the herbs, garlic and lemon zest in a food processor and pulse until roughly chopped. Add the bread and process until a chunky crumb is achieved.

Place lamb chops on a rack above a baking tin and cook for 5 mins. Remove from oven and smear the chops with the Dijon mustard. Divide the herb crust evenly and cook for a further 7 or 8 mins until the crust is golden brown. If you prefer your lamb to be more well cooked, reduce the oven temperature to 170°C and increase the cooking time by 5 mins.

Great served with a wholegrain mustard, mash, and buttered purple sprouting broccoli. Serves 4.

Orange Panna Cotta

15 fl oz (300ml) double cream
3 fl oz (75ml) milk
4 ½ (125gms) caster sugar
zest and juice of 1 large orange or
2 small ones
1½ sachets powdered gelatine/or
2 leaves

Place milk, cream zest and caster sugar in a saucepan and heat until just below boiling point. You will know when it is hot enough when small bubbles appear at the edge of the saucepan.

While the milk and cream mixture is heating, put the orange juice in a shallow dish and sprinkle over the gelatine. Leave to stand for a few mins so that the gelatine dissolves.

When the milk and cream mixture is nearly boiling, remove from the heat and carefully pour in the orange juice and gelatine. Stir to mix everything together and leave for 5 mins to cool slightly.

Pour into individual pudding moulds and leave to set in the refrigerator overnight. Serves 6.

Pan-Fried Tomatoes with Herbs and Smoked Garlic

Terrific served with grilled meats or as a simple starter.

8 tomatoes
4 cloves of smoked garlic
2 oz (50 gm) butter
2 tbsp good olive oil, pinch of salt
masses of freshly ground black pepper
1 tbsp each of freshly chopped, basil, sorrel, marjoram, dill, mint and parsley

Cut the tomatoes in half. Remove the papery skins from the garlic and finely chop. Melt the butter and oil in a frying pan large enough to take all the tomatoes. When the butter has melted add the tomatoes to the pan flat sides facing downwards and the chopped garlic. Add the pinch of salt and as much black pepper as you have patience to grind. Cook the tomatoes very slowly so that they don't singe and the garlic doesn't brown. After about 8 mins turn the tomatoes over and add the chopped herbs and more black pepper. Cook gently for a further 8 mins until the tomatoes are cooked and the herbs have wilted. Serve straight from the pan. Serves 4.

Fish and Shellfish

F ish is highly nutritious and healthy as well as being low in saturated fats. When shopping always try to buy the whole fish rather than fillets or steaks. That way you can see what sort of condition it is in. Generally, eyes should be bright and slightly protruding. The scales tend to come off ultra fresh fish very easily. Its body should be firm, almost stiff, definitely not floppy. White fish should be very white and not showing tinges of brown discoloration. All fish should smell of the sea and not at all "fishy".

At home we tend to avoid serving fish both as a starter and main course, yet if you go to a seafood restaurant this is difficult to avoid. As long as the type of fish used and the sauce served have different characteristics, there's absolutely nothing wrong in serving fish twice.

Plaice Olives with Mussels and Summer Tomato Sauce

3 or 4 fillets of plaice per person depending on the size
4 oz (110gm) smoked mussels
2 oz (50gm) cream cheese, butter
1 lb (450 gm) tomatoes, skinned (optional) and chopped
2 cloves of garlic, crushed in ½ tspn salt
lots of black pepper
2 tbsp olive oil
1 small finely chopped onion
1 tbls tomato purée
2 tbls freshly chopped oregano or marjoram
¼ pt (150ml) white wine
1 tbsp black olives in oil, stoned and coarsely chopped

Remove the skin from the plaice fillets. Chop the smoked mussels and mix with the cream cheese. Spread this mixture on the plaice fillets then roll them up. Put the plaice rolls in a baking dish. Dot with plenty of butter, cover with tin foil and bake for 30 mins in a hot oven 425°F/220°C/ Gas Mark 7.

Meanwhile make the sauce. Put the olive oil in a frying pan. Add the onion and garlic and sâuté slowly for 5 mins to soften the onion. Add the rest of the ingredients. Stir well and simmer gently for 30 mins until a sauce forms. If it gets too dry add a drop of water.

Serve the sauce with the plaice fillets and a crisp green salad. Serves 4.

Bembridge Prawns

*U*nique to the Isle of Wight Bembridge prawns have the most delicate, deep, coral pink markings. They are caught just outside Bembridge harbour by only a few local fishermen. They are rather rare little shellfish and sadly their season is short. In fact, some years we don't see them at all as the tiny coveted catch is relished only by those who fish for them.

Pretty but small, Bembridge prawns are best served in their shell with a lightly-flavoured dip or dressing; such as a herb and mustard mayonnaise or fromage frais flavoured with puréed cucumber or softened and puréed red peppers.

Another simple dish is Bembridge prawns in aromatic butter. Melt about 4 oz (110gm) butter in a frying pan. Add ½ level tspn each of ground black pepper, ground mace and cayenne pepper, two thick slices of lemon, 1 tbls each of chopped fresh parsley, dill and coriander, and 4 tbls white wine. Bubble for 2 minutes then add 2 lb (900gm) shell on prawns. Simmer for a few minutes until the prawns are just heated through then serve immediately with fresh crusty bread to mop up the delicious juices.

Because of their rarity they are something of a luxury item, but it is worth buying a quarter simply to garnish a seafood platter or other special seafood dish. Look out for them during the month of August at Blakes Beach Hut in Ventnor and Captain Stan at Bembridge.

Bembridge Prawns with Coronation Dip

The Coronation Dip is a simplified version of the highly sophisticated sauce that was created in honour of the Coronation of Queen Elizabeth II in 1953. It makes a perfect accompaniment to these tiny crustaceans.

1 lb (450 gm) Bembridge prawns in their shell
juice of one lemon
tabasco sauce according to taste
2 tbsp mayonnaise
1 small carton soured cream
1 chopped beef tomato
1 small, finely diced red pepper
1 chopped shallot, 2 tbsp oil
1 tbls sweet mango pickle
1 tbls mild curry paste

Toss the prawns in the lemon juice and Tabasco and refrigerate until ready to serve.

Heat the oil in the pan and gently cook the shallot, red pepper and tomato until they are soft and pulpy. Add the mango pickle and curry paste. Gently cook together for 5-6 mins. Add the soured cream. Stir thoroughly for one minute. Put this sauce in a processor or liquidizer and blend until smooth. Pass through a sieve, then when cool stir in the mayonnaise. Chill before serving with the prawns, which can be arranged on a bed of crisp lettuce. Serves 4.

Newtown Oysters

*I*t seems that the Romans, during their occupation of the Island, were particularly partial to oysters. Archaeological digs have uncovered a vast quantity of oyster shells in the vicinity of Roman villas.

In 1845 the Corporation of Newport owned seventy-nine acres of oyster beds that were leased out to local fishermen. Unfortunately, over the years the oysters became diseased due to the increased amount of sewage that was released into the River Medina, and by 1870 Island fishmongers were refusing to sell them. Such problems became a thing of the past and Isle of Wight oysters were again being harvested from the beds in Newtown Creek during the 1970's and 1980's, when they became extremely popular. Sadly the fisheries are once again closed.

Newtown Oyster Stew

½ dozen oysters per person
2 shallots, finely chopped
1 oz (25gm) butter,
1 tbls oil
1 clove of garlic, crushed in 1 tspn of salt
small sachet of saffron powder
10 fl oz (275ml) carton of soured cream
1 tbls lemon juice
2 or 3 dashes of Tabasco sauce
¼ pt (150ml) white wine
1 tbsp freshly chopped tarragon
1 carrot, cut into fine matchsticks
2 inch piece of cucumber, cut into fine matchsticks

Carefully open the oysters over a bowl to capture all the escaping juices. Put to one side.

Soften the shallot in the oil and butter. Do not allow to brown. Add the white wine, lemon juice, Tabasco, saffron, tarragon, crushed garlic, and the oyster juice. Simmer for about 5 mins to suffuse the flavours. Add the cream and the carrot and cucumber. Simmer for about 10 minutes until a thin sauce forms.

Two mins before serving add the oysters. They require only the briefest cooking.

Serve in soup plates, garnished with fresh herbs and a half oyster shell filled with extra soured cream seasoned with salt, black and cayenne pepper and a few grains of lumpfish roe.

The Mackerel Fair

*B*efore the First World War the Mackerel Fair was a regular
annual event to celebrate the first mackerel catch of the
season. In those days shoals of mackerel filled the bays of the
South Wight and proved to be an easy catch, unlike today,
when mackerel is caught out at sea. In those days they were
gathered in baskets from the shoreline.

At the beginning of the season a look-out was posted on top
of the cliffs of Whale Bay—named so because of a whale once
stranded there—looking for signs of the first shoal to come the
Island's way. As soon as he saw a blanket of fish darkening the
water he would alert the waiting fishermen who immediately put
out to sea in small boats. A long seine-net was dragged behind
the boat in a large arc around the back of the shoal and then
came back inland. The fish, once contained within the arc, were
then pulled into the shoreline where they were gathered up in
wicker baskets. There was a race as to who would deliver the
first basket of fish to the village, and much jollity ensued.

After the war the mackerel shoals began to dwindle and so,
sadly, did the Mackerel Fair. in June 1986 it was resurrected in
Chale village and once again it became a popular annual event.
To commemorate the first mackerel run of the season the local
harriers put on a paper chase to the local village. Sadly in 2007
the fair no longer takes place.

Lime and Ginger Soused Mackerel

Soused mackerel, and indeed her-rings, can be vinegary, this version is amenable to today's modern tastes.

4 small very fresh whole mackerel
1 small bulb fennel
1 onion, thinly sliced
juice and grated rind of 1 lime
1 inch (2.5cm) piece root ginger, grated
I tspn whole mixed spice
1 fennel bulb, thinly sliced
1 or 2 fresh green chilli peppers, deseeded and finely sliced
1 tbls white wine vinegar
1 tspn honey
salt and pepper

Arrange the thinly sliced fennel and onion on the bottom of a shallow casserole dish (large enough to take the fish lying down).

Thoroughly clean the mackerel under cold run-ning water and pat dry with kitchen paper. Lay them on top of the vegetables.

Put the lime juice and peel, grated root ginger, mixed spice, green chillies, white wine vinegar and honey in a saucepan with ½ pt (275ml) water. Bring to the boil then immediately turn off and stand for 15 mins to cool and infuse.

Pour over the mackerel. Cover with a piece of greased foil or casserole lid then put in a pre-heated oven Gas 5/375°F/190°C for 20 mins. Re-move from the oven and leave to cool slowly in their own juices. Put in the fridge still in their own juices until ready to serve.

To serve: remove the fillets of mackerel from the bones and arrange on plates with some of the marinated vegetables. Serve with new potatoes, crisp salad and caper mayonnaise.

BBQ Mackerel

Many, many years ago when it was a new adventurous place to go I was in Morocco visiting a fish-ing Village on the edge of the At-lantic Ocean. A ship had just ar-rived with its catch of mackerel which was spilling all over the quay-side. There was also a group of Arab men manning huge BBQ's made out of oil drums. For 10 dir-hams (about 10 pence) we could have 6 baby mackerel complete with head and intestines. They came on a plate—that had been wipes clean with paper after the previous customer—with a hunk of freshly baked flat bread and a wedge of sweet juicy lemon. Eat-

ing implements were fingers—my own of course. I have to say it is **THE** most memorable meals I have ever had in my entire life. Simple, perfectly fresh and perfectly cooked.

The trick is that this is one fish that benefits from over-cooking. BBQ over hot embers until the skin is really crisp and brown and the flesh is steaming hot inside—wonderful.

Parsley Stuffed Ham

I love this dish. While it is cooking the aromas are truly mouth-watering. Serve as a light luncheon dish or as a starter.

4 lb (1.8kg) (approx) of Isle of Wight ham, green or smoked (you can use any cut)
4 oz (110gm) freshly chopped parsley (stalks can also be used)
3 cloves garlic
1 tbls crushed black peppercorns

Wash the parsley then blend in a processor with the garlic until fairly fine in texture.

Unwrap your piece of ham and remove the strings or elastic stocking holding it together.

If using smoked ham or locally cured ham, soak in cold water for 40 minutes to remove any excess salt. Flatten out the ham, or if a whole piece cut it almost in half down its length, (do not cut completely in half), then open out. Spread the parsley mixture over the opened out ham then roll up like a Swiss roll. Re-tie the ham or pull back on its elastic stocking.

There are three ways of cooking this ham but in all cases weigh the ham to calculate the cooking time.

Place the ham on the trivet in a pressure cooker. Half cover with water. Use all the weights and cook according to the pressure cooker instructions. Once brought to pressure lower the heat and cook for 10 mins per lb (450gm). New pressure cookers will perform better and take less time.

Place in a roasting bag, squeeze out the air and tie up. Put in a saucepan of cold water and bring to the boil. Reduce the heat and boil for 20 minutes per lb (450gm).

Cover the ham with tin foil, place in a roasting tin and bake in the oven for 15 minutes per lb (450gm) plus an extra 15 minutes.

To test all the methods for 'doneness' insert a long skewer into the centre. If there is no resistance then the ham is cooked. NB. Ham doesn't take as long to cook as many people may think. To finish: remove the skin and some of the fat and roll in freshly chopped parsley. Serve cold.

Tomato and Dill Soup

Tomatoes feature so strongly on the Island. They are grown in the Arreton Valley in huge greenhouses and are available virtually all year round in the supermarkets but look out for them at the Garlic Festival.

2 lb (900gm) ripe tomatoes (cut in half)
1 large tin plum tomatoes
2 large onions (peeled and sliced)
1 oz (25gm) fresh dill
2 vegetable or chicken stock cubes
salt and pepper
2 sugar lumps
2 tbls double cream
1 oz (25gm) butter and 2 tbls oil

Heat the oil and butter in a large saucepan and add the onions. Place over a fairly low heat and cover. Cook gently until the onions are soft and translucent. They must not brown. Add the fresh tomatoes, the tin of tomatoes, stock cubes, salt and pepper and sugar lumps. Cover the pan and simmer until a soft pulp has formed. About 25 mins.

Blend the tomato soup and pass through a sieve to remove the tomato skins and seeds. Return the sieved tomato soup to the pan. Chop the dill and add to the soup. Bring to the boil and simmer for 2-3 mins. If the sauce is too thick add a drop of water. But remember too much water dilutes the flavour. Add the cream and serve.

(For additional flavour add a thinly pared strip of orange peel to the soup when reheating.)

Summer Flan with Basil

6 oz (175gm) short crust pastry
400gm tin chopped tomatoes
1 lb (450gm) very ripe fresh tomatoes (skinned, seeded and chopped)
1 hpd tbls fresh basil (chopped)
1 tbls olive oil
1 medium onion (sliced)
I clove garlic (crushed)
2 courgettes 1" thick (thinly sliced)
1 small red and I small yellow pepper
½ oz (12gm) grated parmesan cheese
½ oz (12gm) sesame seeds
salt and black pepper

Line a flan ring with the pastry. Put in fridge until ready to use.

Heat the oil in a pan and soften the garlic and onion. Add the tomatoes and basil and cook for 5 more mins. Season with salt and pepper. When the mixture has cooled spread over the flan case. Arrange the thinly sliced courgettes in a circle on top of the tomato mixture and 1" (2.5 cm) in from the edge.

Brush the peppers with olive oil and grill. Cut into thin strips and pile in the center of the tart. Season the top lightly.

Sprinkle the top with the parmesan cheeses and sesame seeds and then bake in a hot oven previously heated to 200°C/400°F/Gas Mark 6 for 30 mins.

Garnish with fresh basil leaves. Serve hot or cold with a mixed leaf salad dressed with a walnut oil and lemon dressing to which you have added 1 tspn pesto sauce. Serves 4-6 people.

Lobster Ragout

This finger licking dish is messy but nice.

4 freshly cooked lobsters, cooked for the minimum amount of time
1 onion, finely chopped
3 or 4 cloves garlic, crushed
1 or 2 hot chilli peppers, de-seeded and finely sliced
1 level tbls turmeric
1 level tbls ground coriander
1 lg tin Italian chopped tomatoes
2 tbls tomato purée
olive oil
½ pt (275ml) dry white wine
salt to taste

Put some olive oil in a large deep-sided frying pan. Add the onion, garlic and chilli pepper. Cook gently until the onion is transparent. Add the turmeric and coriander and more oil if necessary and fry for about 3 mins.

To the frying pan add the tinned tomatoes, the tomato purée and the white wine. Simmer until a rich sauce forms. Add water if it becomes too thick. Season to taste.

Remove the claws from the lobster and crack open but keep intact. Remove the head from the lobster and poke out as much coral as you can. With a sharp, heavy knife, cut the tail meat through the shells into 1 inch (2.5cm) thick pieces.

Add the lobster meat with the shells to the simmering sauce. Cook gently for about 8 mins or until the lobster meat is heated through. Arrange on large hot plates and sprinkle with chopped coriander leaves. Serve with lobster picks, plenty of napkins and finger bowls filled with tepid water. Serve with a side dish of noodles. Serves 4.

Lobster Risotto

One 2 lb (900 gm) live lobster
¼ pt (150ml) white wine
8 oz (225gm) arborio rice
2 crushed cloves garlic
2 finely chopped shallots
2 oz (50gm) butter
grated rind and juice of 1 lemon
2 tbls chopped parsley
2 tbls double cream
salt and black pepper

Cook the lobster in two pints (1.1ltr) vegetable stock for 12 mins. Cool. Remove meat from shell and coarsely chop.

Simmer the lobster shells in the cooking water for ½ hour. Strain and keep the stock hot by the side of the risotto pan. (A large heavy-bottomed saucepan or frying pan will do.) Soften the onion and garlic in the butter. Do not brown. Then add the rice and stir round until it becomes transparent. Add the wine and stir until absorbed. Gradually add the simmering lobster stock until it is all absorbed and the rice is cooked. This will take 20-30 mins. Please note that risotto should be wet. Season. Add the lemon juice, the finely grated lemon peel and the cream. Heat through. Then add the lobster meat, and reheat through for 2-3 mins. Serves 4.

Wight Seafood Stew with Samphire

Also known as glasswort, samphire grows in brackish water, and can be collected during July and August in the many little estuaries found all over the Island. There is a certain knack to eating it. Firstly, like asparagus it should be eaten with the hands. Bite on the thin hard thread that runs through its center and pull the flesh off with your teeth. And as with asparagus, lashings of butter are essential.

A selection of locally caught fish to make up 1¼ lb (550gm) of meat. For example:
1 large lobster, shelled
8 oz (225gm) Bembridge prawns, shelled
12 oz (350gm) piece of sea bass, unskinned and cut into 1 inch cubes
4 small plaice fillets, rolled up and secured with a cocktail stick
2 oz (50gm) crab meat,
1 cuttlefish cut into rings
(other kinds of fish can be used but they should all be cut, more or less into bite sized pieces)
1 onion, finely chopped
1 oz (25gm) butter and 1 tbls oil
the juice and finely grated rind of 1 orange
the juice and finely grated rind of 1 lemon
½ pt (275ml) dry white wine
1 tbls freshly chopped parsley
1 tbls freshly chopped dill weed
1 tbls freshly chopped sorrel leaves
piece of lemon grass, finely chopped without the woody bit,
salt and pepper
¼ tspn ground coriander seeds
½ pt (275ml) single cream

½ pt (275ml) fish stock made with the lobster shell, prawn shells and any trimmings from the fish. N.B. fish stock should never be cooked for more than 30 minutes, after this its flavour can become bitter
12 oz (350gm) samphire

Soften the onion in the butter in a pan large enough to eventually take all the listed ingredients.

Add the lemon juice and rind, the orange juice and rind, white wine, lemon grass, coriander and fish stock. Simmer rapidly for 15-20 min until reduced by half.

Add the cream and simmer for a further 10 mins. At this stage the recipe can be put on hold until 5 minutes before you want to serve it.

To the simmering sauce add the herbs then the fish in this order: first the firm fish such as sea bass, salmon, cod, haddock, second the more delicate fish such as sole and plaice unless it is rolled up then add this first, next cuttlefish rings which only require a minute's cooking, and finally anything that has been precooked, such as lobster and prawns that need nothing more than reheating.

Prepare the samphire by washing well in lots of clean running water. Trim off any woody ends. Bring a large pan of salted water to the boil then plunge in the samphire and simmer rapidly for about 8 mins until tender. Drain. Toss in butter or olive oil.

Arrange the samphire in the centre of soup plates and surround with the delicious fish stew.

For a less fattening dish, replace the cream with skimmed milk mixed into 2 tspn of cornflour and add at the same time as the stock and fruit juice etc. Serves 4

Lobster and Salmon Pie with Red Pepper Sauce

Most recipes call for lobster to be reheated. It is therefore essential that you don't overcook it in the first place. If I am making lobster ravioli or a pie, I cook a 1 lb lobster for a mere 5 mins, just long enough to firm up the flesh, and make it easy to handle.

two 1 lb (450gm) lobsters
8 oz (225gm) of fresh salmon — the tail-piece will do for this recipe if it's cheaper
1 tbsp fresh chopped dill weed or mint
¼ pt (150ml) double cream
1 red pepper, thinly sliced then cut into 1 inch l2.5cm) lengths
lots of black pepper and a generous pinch of salt
8 oz (225gm) shortcrust pastry

Soften the red pepper in a little oil until soft, then cool. Cook the lobsters in lots of boiling water for 5 mins. Remove the lobster meat from the shells and cut into large dice. Remove the skin from the salmon and purée in the blender. Remove the salmon from the blender and add the dill weed or mint and the cream. Mix to a smooth paste then add the diced lobster and the red pepper.

Divide the pastry in half and roll out each half to fit into a 7 inch (18cm) flan ring. Turn the salmon and lobster mixture into the pastry-lined flan ring and cover with the rest of the pastry rolled out as thinly as possible.

Bake in a preheated oven, 425°F/220°C/Gas Mark 7, for 30 mins. Serve hot or cold with a crisp salad and red pepper sauce (see recipe below). Serves 4.

Red Pepper Sauce

1 large diced red pepper
1 small clove of garlic
1 small onion, diced
2 ripe tomatoes, quartered
2 tbls olive oil
1 small carton of soured cream
salt and pepper and Tabasco

Soften the red pepper, garlic, onion and tomato very slowly in the oil until a thick pulp is formed. Press through a sieve and when cold stir into the soured cream. Season with the salt, pepper and Tabasco, and serve hot or chilled.

Fur Game

Rabbits (then called Coney) were first introduced to the Island in 1225. Bowcombe Manor even employed a keeper of conies who successfully sold around 200 skins per year. Coney-garths (stone walled enclosures) were built at Bowcombe and on many other estates to keep the burrowing rabbits in. By the 15th century they were so profitable that rabbit groves were taken into account when land leases were granted. Inevitably the Island became over-run and little was done to check their numbers until 1845 when foxes were introduced mainly for sporting purposes

Unlike the rabbit, the hare is indigenous to the Island. Sadly their numbers are declining, being sometimes indiscriminately shot during their breeding season which curtails the rearing of future generations.

Hare is a deliciously dark, robust meat that can be married with other strong flavours. To be sure of future supplies it should only be bought during its season which runs from August to February. Any other time be prudent and refuse to buy it.

The discovery of venison bones on archaeological digs provides evidence that deer was first reared on the Island during the Roman occupation.

Much later during the Isabella de Fortibus ownership of the Island, deer was hunted in Parkhurst Forest and reared in the parklands surrounding Appledurcombe House.

In the 1980s deer was for a short time, once again introduced to the Island.

Wild rabbit and hare can be purchased from Island butchers October onwards when the first pheasants are shot.

Breast of Chicken with Cider and I of W Blue Cheese Sauce

4 chicken breasts (Isle of Wight)
2 tbsp oil
1 oz (25gm) butter
¼ pt (150ml) dry I of W cider,
salt and pepper, pinch of cayenne
pepper
1 garlic clove, crushed
3 oz (75gm) I of W Blue cheese
¼ pt (150ml) chicken stock
4 tbls double cream

Make sure all the bones are removed from the chicken breasts. Arrange them in a shallow roasting tin, brush with the oil and season with salt, pepper and cayenne pepper. Place in a hot oven, 450°F/230°C/Gas Mark 8, and roast for 15 mins. By this stage they should be cooked but still moist.

Meanwhile make the sauce. Melt the butter in a sauté pan then add the crushed garlic and soften. Add the stock, cider, cream and cheese and simmer until a thick sauce develops. Add salt and pepper and cayenne pepper to taste. Add the pan juices from the chicken. If the sauce is too thick add a drop more stock. Serve the sauce with the chicken. Goes well with pasta or new buttery potatoes. Serves 4.

Summer Pudding

*I*f any pudding deserves the name "Queen of Puddings" it should have been this. It is all British and something we have every right to be proud of.

Living on the Island we are lucky there are so many fruit growers to supply us with all the soft fruits we could possibly need to make this delightful dessert.

There are few things nicer than spending a warm Saturday morning foraging in a self-pick farm for the fruits, then an idle Saturday afternoon making it—and on an even lazier Sunday afternoon eating it.

Any sort of soft fruit can be used, but it is essential that blackcurrants or redcurrants, or both, are included. This is because a certain amount of natural pectin is needed to seep from the berries to give the rich red juice a slight setting quality.

Traditionally, Summer Pudding was made in a creamy-white, crock pudding basin The basin is lined with thin slices of very good fresh bread (not white sliced), crusts removed. The basin is then filled to the brim with the luscious red berry mixture then a lid of more thinly sliced bread is squashed on top then covered with greaseproof paper and weighed down overnight, giving time for the juices to soak into the bread.It is now trendy to serve individual Summer Puddings with raspberry coulis.

Coconut Mousse with Strawberry Sauce

Coconut and strawberries are an unusual but inspired blend.

14 oz (400gm) can of condensed milk
8 oz (225gm) desiccated coconut
small tub Greek, strained yoghurt
1 sachet gelatine
3 egg whites
8 oz (225gm) strawberries
3 oz (75gm) castor sugar

Blend the coconut and the condensed milk together. Stand for 1 hour to soften the coconut. Sprinkle the gelatine over 3 tbsp cold water. Stand a few minutes until swollen then heat in a double saucepan or in a microwave until the crystals are dissolved. Whisk the egg whites to stiff peaks. Add the yoghurt to the coconut-flavoured milk, then quickly beat in the softened gelatine. Mix quickly before the gelatine has a chance to form strings. (Keeping the coconut mixture at room temperature will help to avoid this problem.) Fold in the beaten egg white and pour into individual or one large dish, that will look pretty when the mousse is turned out.

Strawberry sauce: Put the sugar in a saucepan with a scant ¼ pt (150ml) water. Dissolve the sugar then simmer rapidly for 5 mins. Put the strawberries in a blender. Pour over the hot syrup and process to a smooth sauce. Push through a fine sieve to remove the tiny pips. Taste and add a dash of lemon juice if necessary.

Turn out the mousse Pour the sauce around and garnish with more strawberries. Serves 8.

Strawberry Shortcake

A simple sweet to make yet because it is—and must be—made with butter, it carries a flavour of some sophistication. Best eaten the same day it is made. Serve in the afternoon with a refreshing cup of Earl Grey tea.

8 oz (225gm) ripe strawberries
clotted or whipped double cream
icing sugar

Shortcake

6 oz (175gm) good quality butter
6 oz (175gm) castor sugar
3 eggs
1 tspn vanilla essence
8 oz (225gm) self-raising flour

Cream together butter and sugar until soft, pale and fluffy. Add vanilla essence. Gradually add the beaten eggs. Add a teaspoon of flour with each addition of egg to prevent curdling (this shouldn't be necessary if the butter is soft enough). Sift the flour, then carefully fold into the creamed mixture. This mixture is quite firm, unlike a sponge mix, so don't be tempted to add any liquid; and don't overwork or the air will be removed.

Divide the mixture between two lightly greased and floured 7-inch (17cm) sandwich tins. Level the mixture then bake in the centre of a moderate oven 350°F/180°C/Gas4, for 25-30 mins. Cool before turning out.

When completely cold, sandwich together with the whipped or clotted cream and sliced strawberries. Dredge with fine icing sugar. Serves 6-8.

Strawberry Ice-Cream

1½ lb (700gm) ripe strawberries
6-8 oz (175-225 gm) castor sugar
(more for a softer ice-cream)
1 pt (570 ml) double cream
3 large eggs, separated
1 tbsp fresh lemon juice

Purée the strawberries and push through a fine hair sieve to remove the tiny pips. Add the lemon juice to the strawberry purée.

Put the egg yolks and half the sugar in a bowl over a saucepan of boiling water. Whisk until thick, pale and creamy. Cool. Whisk the cream to peaks. Whisk the egg white into peaks. Add the remaining sugar to the egg whites and whisk until stiff.

Fold the now cold egg yolk mixture into the whipped cream. Then fold in the strawberry purée. Finally fold in the egg whites. Pour into a shallow container and freeze. If the ice-cream freezes too hard to serve, transfer to the fridge ½ hour before serving. Serves 4-6.

Strawberry and Lemon Roulade with Rose-Scented Sauce

A stupendous dinner party dessert, or serve with afternoon tea on the lawn.

3 large eggs
4 oz (110gm) castor sugar
3 oz (75gm) ground almonds
½ oz (10gm) fine cake or digestive biscuit crumbs

Filling and Sauce
½ pt (275ml) double cream
1 tbls lemon curd, 1 lb (450gm) strawberries
1 tbls triple distilled rosewater
3-4 oz (75-110gm) castor sugar

Line a Swiss roll tin with buttered greaseproof paper and scatter finely with the cake crumbs. Whisk together the eggs and sugar until thick and creamy. Very gently fold in the ground almonds. Spread this mixture evenly, over the Swiss roll tin. Bake near the top of the oven for 12 mins, 375°F/190°C/Gas5, until just firm. Turn out onto a sheet of paper sprinkled with sugar while still warm. Place another piece of greaseproof paper on top then roll up Swiss roll fashion. (If you don't do this the cake may crack when it is filled with cream and finally rolled up. Some people prefer this effect.)

Whip the cream with the lemon curd. Chop half the strawberries and fold into the cream. Unroll the cold sponge and spread with the lemon and strawberry cream. Roll up again and dredge with icing sugar.

To make the sauce, put the sugar in a saucepan with 4 tbls water and the rosewater. Dissolve the sugar, then simmer rapidly for 5 mins. Put this syrup with the strawberries in a blender and purée. Sieve out the tiny strawberry pips.

To serve, trim away the coarse ends of the roulade. Cut 1 inch (2.5cm) thick slices. Lay in the centre of individual plates. Pour the sauce around and garnish with more strawberries and tiny pink rose petals. Serves 6.

Quick Strawberry Meringue

Serve in pretty, but heat-proof dishes. Children will love it too.

1 lb (450gm) strawberries, thickly sliced
6 oz (175gm) castor sugar
2 tbls Grand Marnier
½ tbls lemon juice
3 large egg whites

Toss the sliced strawberries in the Grand Marnier, the lemon juice and 2 oz (50gm) of the sugar. Divide between 4 dishes. Whisk the egg whites to stiff peaks, then whisk in the remaining castor sugar. Heat the grill. Pile the meringue on top of the strawberries. Place on the grill tray and slide under the grill. Have the dishes as far away from the flame/element as possible. At this stage watch the dessert like a hawk, it burns quickly. As soon as the meringue begins to turn a golden brown colour it is ready to serve. Serves 4.

Red Berry Jelly with Raspberry Sauce

The Cider Barn at Godshill, as well as cider, has a fascinating range of old English fruit wines.

1 pt (570ml) strawberry wine
1 lb (450gm) mixed red berries i.e. raspberries, strawberries, redcurrants, blackcurrants, blueberries, loganberries
4 oz (110gm) castor sugar1 sachet plus an extra tspn of gelatine

Raspberry sauce
8 oz (225gm) raspberries
4 oz (110gm) icing sugar
juice of 1 lemon

Gently heat half of the strawberry wine with the sugar until the sugar has dissolved (don't over heat or it will lose its flavour). Soften the gelatine in 3 tbsp cold water, then heat to dissolve. Stir into the warm sweetened wine. Add the washed fruit to the warm wine, then the remaining cold wine. Pour into a jelly mould. Cover and set in the fridge, preferably overnight.

To make the sauce, put the raspberries, icing sugar and lemon juice into a processor and blend until smooth. Pass through a sieve to remove the raspberry pips. Keep cool until ready to serve.

I like to set the jelly in an oblong terrine then cut thick slices and serve surrounded with the sauce and garnished with extra summer berries.

Three courses from the kitchen of Fultons Seafood and Chop House

Spicy Bembridge Crab-cakes

1 lb (450gm) picked 50/50 Bembridge crab meat
4 oz (110gm) grated ginger
5 chopped chillies
small handful coriander
small handful basil
zest of 4 limes
2 lb (900gm) mashed potato
pinch of salt and pepper
1 bunch of chopped spring onions

breadcrumbs
eggs
flour

Mix all ingredients together and shape into small cakes. Coat with flour, then beaten egg and roll in breadcrumbs, ensuring an even coating is achieved.

Pan fry for 3-4 mins on each side or place on oven tray in <u>hot oven</u> (180°C) for 8-10 mins.

Beer Battered Cod Loin with Creamed Minted Peas

6-8 oz (225gm) cod loin
½ pint (275ml) of good ale
4-5 oz (110gm) flour (roughly)
salt and pepper
5-6 oz frozen peas
5 fl oz cream
salt and pepper
small bunch fresh mint

Mix together ale and flour to make a thick batter. Mix in salt and pepper. Dust cod loin in flour. Place in batter, then remove and allow excess to drain. Place carefully into deep fat fryer (180°C) and allow to cook for 6-8 mins. Remove and drain on kitchen paper.

Bring cream, peas, salt and pepper to boil. Place into a food processor. Blitz into a smooth paste, add mint, blitz again, remove and serve.

Spiced Berry Crème Brulée

Brulée

2 pints (1.1ltr) of cream
10 egg yolks
3 oz (75gm) caster sugar
1 vanilla pod

Berries
1 bag of frozen summer berries
2 tbls cinnamon
3 oz (75gm) caster sugar

Mix egg yolks, sugar and vanilla seeds together. Bring cream and used vanilla pod to the boil. Pour onto egg mix. Keep whisking, return to the pan and place on a low heat until mixture slowly thickens (about 10 mins).

Berries
Place ingredients in pan and bring to the boil, remove and allow to cool. Place a spoonful in the bottom of ramekins then pour over the brulée mix. Allow to chill in fridge. When ready to serve sprinkle with demerera sugar and place under a hot grill for 2-3 mins. Allow to cool for 30 secs then serve.
Makes 6-8

Food from the Hedgerow

Spring tends to arrive on the Isle of Wight earlier than the rest of the country, consequently our hedgerow crops come to fruition earlier too. It is not unknown to be picking blackberries at the end of August.

When gathering blackberries or any other hedgerow fruit for that matter, try to avoid roadside hedges. Throughout the summer they have been barraged with dirt, dust, and an inexhaustible supply of car fumes. The Island is woven with a maze of twisting and winding public footpaths and bridle ways, all crossing fertile farm-land, pasture land and National Trust land. This makes it easy to get away from the verges and harvest a basket full of fruit that hasn't been tainted by the busy traffic.

While out and about keep an eye open for cob-nuts and that Christmas favourite, sweet chestnuts. Unfortunately the whereabouts of such trees are a closely guarded secret. However, try searching them out in the broad-leaved woodlands the Island is so lucky to have. Sweet chestnuts are the ones with the hairy outer shell the other type are for conker contests.

Other useful fruits to look out for are sloes, crab apples and rosehips. And elderberries should be prolific providing all the elderflowers weren't picked in the late spring to make elderflower sorbet, jam, wine etc.

With the exception of blackberries, hedgerow fruits are very sour and require more sugar than normal fruits. They are however, because of their high pectin content, excellent for making Victorian-style jellies to go with meat and game, and the often underrated English fruit wines.

Terrine of Baby Leeks

Strictly speaking, leeks are a winter vegetable, so this terrine is best made at the beginning of the season when the leeks are still tiny (no more than ½ inch thick).

2 lb (900gm) baby leeks
salt and lots of black pepper
1 small finely chopped clove of garlic
1 tbsp finely chopped fresh thyme or sage

Dressing: 4 tbls olive oil,
1 tbls white wine vinegar
1 tbls tarragon mustard,
pinch of sugar
1 tspn of lightly crushed white mustard seeds

Trim and clean the leeks, but leave as much of the green part as possible intact. Place the leeks in a colander over a pan of simmering water or steamer and steam until tender.

Mix together the garlic and chopped herb. Lightly oil a 1 pint (570ml) terrine and arrange a layer of leeks on the bottom. Season with salt, pepper, and some of the garlic and herbs. Continue these layers until all the leeks are used up. Make sure the layers are alternated in such a way that you have the green part of the leek at both ends of the terrine. The leeks should come up above the top of the terrine. Cover with cling-film or foil then weight down to compress the leeks. Put in the fridge still weighed down and leave overnight to chill.

To serve, put the dressing ingredients in a jar and shake together. Carefully turn out the leek terrine and with a very sharp knife cut ½ inch (1cm) thick slices. Still handling the terrine carefully lay one or two slices on a plate and pour some of the mustard dressing over the top. Serves 4.

Marinated Mushrooms

a generous 1 lb (450gm) mushrooms
1 small onion, finely chopped
2 cloves of garlic, crushed in a tspn of salt
juice of 1 lemon
4 tbsp olive oil
¼ pt (150ml) red wine
black pepper
2 tbls freshly chopped parsley

Wash and dry the mushrooms. Slice thickly then toss in the lemon juice. Heat the olive oil in a pan and gently fry the mushrooms and onions for 15 mins. Add the crushed garlic, black pepper, red wine and parsley and cook gently for a further 5 minutes. Serve cold with cold meats and pates. Serves 4

Potato, Garlic and Wight Wine Soup

Isle of Wight garlic is internationally renowned, and this silky, smooth, cream soup, slightly sweetened by the wine, does it great justice. Serve piping hot with garlic and parsley croutons. A must for any autumn dinner party.

1 lb (450gm) potatoes
2 large onions
½ pt (275ml) dry or medium white wine
10-12 skinned garlic cloves
1 pt (570ml) vegetable or chicken stock
oil for frying
2 tbls fresh chopped parsley
salt and black pepper
soured cream and paprika to garnish

Finely slice the onions. Peel and dice the potatoes. Put the onion and potato in a heavy-bottomed saucepan with the garlic, and about 4 tbls oil. Cover with a lid and simmer very gently until the vegetables are soft and mushy. It is essential that the vegetables do not brown. Add the wine and stock and simmer for 20 mins. Purée the contents of the pan to a smooth consistency. Check seasoning. Add the parsley if using. Reheat and serve garnished with the soured cream and paprika, and garlic croutons. If the consistency is too thick add a drop more stock or wine. Serves 4.

Garlic Croutons

Cut a stale French stick into thin ¼ inch (½ cm) slices. Place on a baking sheet in a low temperature oven to dry out. In a processor blend together 2 cloves of garlic, 2 tbls of olive oil, and a large bunch of fresh parsley. Spoon this sauce on top of the crisp croutons and arrange on top of the soup with the dollops of soured cream.

A great alternative is to replace potatoes with Jerusalem artichokes.

Pheasant in Godshill Barn Cider with Apple Cakes

In the thirteenth century cider-making took place at Wootton Manor. Today a good strong cider can be bought at the Cider Barn in Godshill along with their many English country wines.

2 small hen pheasants
½ pt (275ml) Godshill dry cider
8 shallots,
4 cloves of garlic,
crushed in salt
2 tspn dried basil or sage
½ pt (275ml) chicken stock
oil,
1 tbsp cornflour

Apple Cakes

1 large crisp dessert apple
1 medium potato,
salt and pepper
1 level tbls dried sage,
½ beaten egg

Put some oil in a large pan and brown the pheasants all over. Take out and put to one side. Skin the shallots, keep whole and lightly brown in the same pan. Add the garlic and cook until pale and golden. Now add the chicken stock, cider, and herbs. Simmer for a couple of minutes to amalgamate the flavours. Place the pheasants in an ovenproof casserole dish. Pour over the cider sauce. Cover with a lid or tin foil and cook in a preheated oven 350°F/180°C/Gas Mark 4 for 1 hour 30 mins. Remove the pheasants from the casserole and keep warm. Mix the cornflour with a drop of water then add to the sauce that the pheasants have been cooking in. Put on the hob and simmer until the sauce thickens. If the dish is not heatproof you will have to transfer the sauce to a saucepan. A drop of cream could be added to enrich the sauce. To serve, remove the legs, and carve the breast meat. Arrange on top of the apple cakes. Serves 4.

Apple Cakes

Grate the apple and potato. Mix together with the seasoning, sage and beaten egg. Heat some oil in a frying pan. Drop in spoonfuls of the mixture and cook slowly for 10 mins. Turn over and cook slowly on the other side for a further 10 mins. The cakes can be precooked and re-heated.

Arable Farming

*I*n the 13th century the fertile Isle of Wight was a prolific supplier of corn, some of which was transported by ship to Scot-
land to feed the soldiers fighting for Edward I against the Scots.
By the time the three month voyage to Berwick was over much
of the corn had gone moldy. Further supplies were lost when
winter sailings proved treacherous and several ships sank.

In the 1790s the Island became a major supplier of wheat and
barley to the south of England. The enthusiasm for wheat production in such quantities was generated by the "No Taxes"'
law, which greatly increased the wealth of the Island farmers.

After a slump in the mid-19th century, farming on the same
scale was never resurrected. Many farms were sold up and
those that remained turned to milk production.

The First World War brought about a shortage of foreign im-
ports and Islanders were encouraged to produce their own food.
Market gardening quickly got under way and a large variety of
seasonal crops were produced.

There are still several water-powered corn mills on the Island—mainly relics of the past—and Neal Smith at Calbourne
Mill continues to produce its own stone-ground flour. It has a
wonderful nutty flavour and makes the most delicious wholemeal bread.

Chicken with Island Wine and Grape Sauce

For this dish I recommend that you use the baby spring chickens.

4 baby chickens
8 oz (225gm) white grapes
1 pt (570ml) Island white wine
2 tbls fresh tarragon
1 level tbsp cornflour,
1 oz (25gm) butter
2 cloves of garlic, crushed in some salt lots of freshly ground black pepper

Place the baby chickens in a roasting pan. Pour over the wine and sprinkle with tarragon, crushed garlic and black pepper. Cover with foil and oven bake for 60 mins.

Test that the chickens are cooked through. If they aren't cook for a little longer. Remove the chickens from the roasting pan and keep warm. Remove the skins and hook out the pips from the grapes if they aren't seedless (fiddly but worth it). Put the pan with all its juices on a ring and raise the heat. Mix the cornflour with a drop of water or wine and stir into the juices. Cook, stirring all the time until the sauce has thickened. Add the grapes, then the butter to enrich the sauce. Cook for a further 4-5 mins, which will be just long enough to heat the grapes through without over-cooking them. Serve the chickens and the sauce with rice and green beans.
Serves 4.

Venison Cutlets with Celeriac Sauce

This is an unusual sauce to serve with venison. The contrasting flavour of celeriac makes a perfect marriage.

8 cutlets taken from the saddle
4 rashers of streaky bacon
1 large celeriac
1 small potato, peeled and halved
juice of 1 lemon
2 cloves of garlic, crushed in a little salt
1 inch (2.5cm) fresh horseradish root, finely grated
¼ pt (150ml) double cream
1 tspn of celery salt and black pepper

Stretch the rashers of bacon, cut in half and wrap around the venison cutlets. Pan fry for 8 mins each side. They are best cooked pink. Meanwhile make the sauce (it can be made in advance). Peel the celeriac, cut into cubes and boil in plenty of salted water with the potato and lemon juice. Drain and put in a blender with the rest of the sauce ingredients. Blend to a smooth purée. Serve immediately with the venison cutlets. Accompany with redcurrant jelly, and braised red cabbage or baby beetroot. Serves 4.

From the menu of
The Royal Hotel

Pan Seared Fresh Scallops Crushed Peas, Creamy Shallot Purée, Sherry Vinegar And Truffle Oil Dressing

3 large scallops per portion.

Gently sweat chopped shallots in little olive oil, add milk just to cover, simmer until soft.

Liquidize in a jug blender and reduce to correct consistency as necessary.

Crush cooked peas with a fork, season and add a little olive oil and sherry vinegar.

Add 1 part sherry vinegar, to 5 parts white truffle oil for the dressing.

Pan fry scallops in smoking hot olive oil, put 3 small rings of peas in middle with scallops on top, put two lines of shallot purée across the plate, garnish scallops with chervil.

Dress the plate with truffle vinaigrette.

Pan Fried Medallions of Veal

sage and parmesan bread-crumbs
sauté new potatoes
caramelized onions
baby capers
lemon and parsley butter

Roast the new potatoes with rosemary, lemon, olive oil and sea salt.

Place a ring of roast new potatoes in the middle of the plate, caramelized onions on top, two sage and parmesan bread crumbed medallions of veal on top.

Place blanched and then caramelized cauliflower around the plate, with buttered broad beans and mange tout halves.

Dress the vegetables with beurre noisette, chopped capers and chopped parsley.

Place two caper berries on top of the veal, and pan-fried quail egg.

Vanilla Roasted Pineapple Malibu Panna Cotta

To serve:

Fresh pineapple
Vanilla panna cotta
Vanilla scented caramel sauce

Cut pineapple into 8 square pieces, removing the core.

Poach the pineapple in vanilla caramel, simmer for 5 mins, turn off heat and leave to cool. Turn out panna cotta onto plate.

Place pineapple next to panna cotta; garnish pineapple with thin strip of sugared vanilla pod.

Sun

Sea

Sand

Sensuality

The Isle of Wight

It's The Only Place To Be

Wood Pigeon with Sloe Gin Sauce

4 plump pigeons
1 onion or 4 shallots, finely chopped
½ pt (275ml) stock made from the pigeon bones
¼ pt (150ml) sloe gin
1 tbls of any herb jelly
1 tspn tomato purée
2 tspn cornflour
lots of freshly ground black pepper, salt

First prepare the pigeons. Remove the legs, then take a sharp knife and split the breasts away from the carcass by cutting in half through the cavity. You should end up with the two breasts attached to the breast bone on one half and the back bone of the bird on the other half. Put the back bone and legs in a saucepan with onions, carrots and your favourite spices. Simmer gently for a couple of hours to make the stock. Place the four pairs of breasts, still connected to the bone, in a roasting tin and smear liberally with butter. Put in a preheated oven 375°F/190°C/Gas Mark 5, for 15-20 mins depending on how well you like them cooked i.e. rare or pink. Well-done roast pigeon will become tough roast pigeon. Meanwhile make the sauce. Soften the onion and lightly brown in a small amount of oil. Add the now strained stock, sloe gin, herb jelly, tomato purée and black peppercorns. Simmer rapidly until reduced by half. Mix the cornflour with a drop of water and add to the sauce. Simmer until thickened. Add the meat juices from the roast pigeon. Season to taste. Either serve the two breasts still on the bone or carefully remove. Slice each one in half to form two petals and fan out onto hot plates, then pour the sauce around the breasts. Serve with creamed potato and braised red cabbage. Serves 4.

Loin of Pork with Caper and Paprika Sauce

4 large chunky Isle of Wight pork loin chops
oil
1 onion, very finely chopped
2 cloves of garlic, crushed in a little salt
1 level tbls tomato puree
1 tbls capers
1 tbls hot paprika
½ pt (275ml) white wine
½ pt (275ml) double cream

Soften the onion and garlic in 2 tbls oil, don't allow to brown. Add the paprika and cook for a couple of mins to take away the rawness of the spice. Add the tomato purée, capers and wine. Simmer rapidly to reduce by half.

Put the chops to grill, fry or barbecue, 8 mins each side or 10 mins for crispy chops.

Add the cream to the reduced sauce and simmer until the sauce thickens. Season to taste and serve with the pork chops. Accompany with broccoli and sâuté potatoes. Serves 4.

Nuggets of Pork with Apple, Sage and Onion Relish

2 large or 3 small fillets of Isle of Wight pork, cut into 2 inch (5cm) thick discs
1 large onion, finely chopped
1 tbls oil
1 oz (25gm) butter
2 peeled and diced cooking apples
1 tbls castor sugar
1 tbls freshly chopped sage
oil for frying
¼ pt (150ml) white wine or chicken stock
1 oz (25gm) cold butter
salt and pepper

First make the relish. Melt the butter and 1 tbls oil in a saucepan. Add the onion and cook slowly until the onion is soft. Add the apple, chopped sage and sugar. Cover the pan with a lid and simmer until the apple has reduced to a pulp. Beat with a fork to blend the ingredients together. Put to one side and keep warm. This sauce can be made in advance and reheated or served cold with cold roast pork.

Heat some oil in a frying pan and add the nuggets of pork. Sâuté for 5 mins each side, until golden and slightly crunchy on the surface. Push the pork to one side and add the wine and butter. Bring to the boil so that a thin glaze forms. Serve the pork immediately. Coat with a little of the glaze and put a spoonful of relish on the side. Serves 4.

Apple Jelly with Blackberry Sauce

Afton Park in Freshwater produces a delicious apple juice, pressed from English Cox and Bramleys, and its flavour is the secret of this lovely fresh jelly.

1 lb (450gm) dessert apples
1 pt (570ml) Afton apple juice
6 oz (175gm) castor sugar
4 tbls Calvados
juice of ½ a lemon
finely pared rind of ½ a lemon
1½ sachets of gelatine

Blackberry Sauce

8 oz (225gm) blackberries
4 oz (110gm) castor sugar
sprig of fresh mint
1 tbls lemon juice

First make the jelly. Peel and core the apples and cut into dice. Put half the apple juice, the sugar, lemon juice, lemon rind and apples in a saucepan and simmer gently until the sugar has dissolved and the apples are tender.

Soften the gelatine in 3 tbls of cold apple juice then heat through to dissolve. Add to the apples in the warm juice. Now add the remaining cold juice and the Calvados. Remove the lemon peel then pour into a jelly mould to set overnight.

Blackberry sauce

Put the blackberries, lemon juice, sprig of mint and castor sugar in a saucepan and simmer until the sugar has dissolved and the blackberries are soft and pulpy. Don't overcook or you will end up with jam. Remove the sprig of mint and pass the fruit through a sieve. Chill before serving.

Turn the jelly into a straight-sided dish and surround with a pool of the blackberry sauce. Serves 6.

Spiced Honey Sauce

Like wine and cheese, the flavour of honey varies depending on where it comes from. The unique flavour of Isle of Wight honey is due to the vast maze of hedgerows that twist and turn around the arable and pasture land.

4 tbls Isle of Wight honey
1 tspn mixed spice
1 tbls chopped walnuts
1 oz (25gm) butter
¼ pt (150ml) double cream

Put all the ingredients in a saucepan and simmer gently for 5 mins, increase the heat and boil for 10 mins. Serve while hot with the Christmas ice cream. The combination of hot and cold is divine.

Damson Wine Jelly with Poached Pears

A perfect dessert to serve after a delicious autumn meal of venison or other game dish.

1 pt (570ml) Damson wine
a piece of orange peel
1 cinnamon stick
2 blades of mace
4 oz (110gm) castor sugar
2 tbls brandy
1 sachet of gelatine crystals
4 ripe pears (but not overripe)

Peel the pears, leaving the small stems intact. Place in a saucepan with half the wine, the orange peel, cinnamon stick, castor sugar, and mace. Put on a gentle heat and poach until the pears are tender and have absorbed the wine flavour. Remove the pears and chill. Strain the remaining wine.

Soften the gelatine in 3 tbls cold water, then heat through until dissolved. Add to the poaching liquid, then add the rest of the damson wine and the brandy. Pour into a jelly mould and refrigerate overnight until set. Serve the jelly with the poached pears and cold whipped cream. Serves 4.

Apple and Marzipan Tart with Red Plum Sauce

This is a very simple dessert with a French influence, and a tribute to Isabella de Fortibus who, in the late 13th century, was the Island's principal landowner and lived in Carisbrooke Castle.

8 oz (225gm) puff pastry
6 oz (175gm) marzipan
2 small or 1 large cooking apple
2 tbsp castor sugar
8 oz (225gm) red plums
6 oz (175gm) castor sugar

Divide the pastry in half and roll out two 8-inch (20cm) circles. Place one onto a baking sheet. Roll out the marzipan to a 7-inch (18cm) circle then place on top of the pastry circle.

Peel and thinly slice the apple and arrange on top of the marzipan, then sprinkle over the sugar. Dampen the edges of the pastry with the beaten egg and place the remaining circle of puff pastry on top of the apples. Seal down the edges. Brush the whole pie with beaten egg, then mark out a pattern on the surface of the pie with a fork. Bake in a preheated oven 425°F/220°C/Gas Mark 7, for 35 mins.

To make the plum sauce, simmer the plums with the sugar until they are pulpy, then pass through a sieve to remove the skins and stones. Serve hot with the pie.

Individual pies can be made in a similar way. They look best when arranged individually on plates in a glistening ruby red puddle of plum sauce. Serves 4.

Three courses from the kitchen of The Crown Inn

Roast Pepper and Courgette Soup

1 oz (25gm) butter or margarine
2 oz (50gm) onion
7 oz (200gm) mixed peppers
7 oz (200gm) courgettes
1¾ pts (1ltr) vegetable stock or water
1 garlic clove chopped
salt, pepper,
chopped parsley,
croutons

Melt the better or margarine in a pan. Add the chopped onion, diced courgettes and garlic, cook for a few minutes. Roast the sliced mixed peppers in a hot oven for about 8 mins. Add the roasted peppers to the pan, continue to cook for a few mins. Add the vegetable stock or water and simmer for 30 mins. Liquidize or pass through a sieve. Return to a clean pan, reheat, season and correct consistency. Serve and sprinkle with chopped parsley.
Serves 4.

Pan-fried Pork Steak with an Apple and Cointreau Sauce

2 oz (50gm) butter or oil
4 x 7oz (200gm) pork steaks
14 oz (400gm) cooking apples
2 oz (50gm) sugar
1 oz (25gm) butter
1 fl oz (25ml) Cointreau

Heat the butter in a frying pan. Lightly season the pork steaks both sides with salt and pepper. Fry the steaks on both sides until done. For the apple and Cointreau, peel, core and wash the apples. Place the apples, butter, sugar and Cointreau in a pan, cook to a purée. Season and correct the consistency. Place pork steaks on warm plates, serve with sauce and garnish with grilled apple segments.
Serves 4.

Crown Inn Deep Bread and Butter Pudding

3½ oz (100gms) sultanas and raisins
11 slices of medium cut white bread
4 medium eggs
3½ oz (100gms) brown sugar
1 tsp vanilla essence
zest of a small orange
scant 1 pt (½ ltr) milk
grated or ground nutmeg

Butter 8 slices of the bread. Cut the crusts off all 11 slices and cut each slice into 4. Lay 3 slices (12 pieces) of the buttered bread on the base of a pie dish butter side down. Sprinkle with half the fruit and zest and a little of the sugar. Place the unbuttered 3 slices of bread on top. Sprinkle with the rest of the fruit, zest and a little of the sugar. Place rest of buttered bread buttered side up on top overlapping the edges. Beat milk, vanilla essence and eggs together and pass through sieve. Pour onto pudding, press down lightly and leave to soak for half an hour. Sprinkle with grated nutmeg and remaining brown sugar. Cook in moderate oven 160°C/300°F/Gas2 or 45 mins until set, and serve.
Serves 6.

Christmas on the Isle of Wight

*I*t would be wrong to think the Isle of Wight closes down after
the summer season. It is true that everyone sits back for a bit
of a breather and to re-stoke the fire, but most are armchair
planning ready for the Christmas festivities to come, then as
soon as November arrives menus are printed and everyone is
set to take the Christmas bookings.

Many hotels offer special three or four day Christmas breaks
and restaurants open their doors for the annual office party and
for Christmas Day and Boxing Day lunch. Local suppliers are
stocking up with lots of festive goodies and for those of us who
find it all too much, the outside caterers are there to give a
helping hand.

In fact, on the Island thoughts for Christmas arrive early and
bookings are often made as soon as August.

Chefs agree that roast turkey with all the trimmings is the
most popular choice of menu, even though most customers will
be eating more of the same on the 25th. Roast turkey is such a
significantly traditional meal it puts everyone in an early party
mood.

If you fancy a change from turkey there are plenty of alterna-
tives such as pheasant, venison, goose, pork, or ribs of beef,
and if you buy at a small local butcher the chances are they will
be locally reared.

Christmas on the Isle of Wight can be a real treat, and that
ferry trip across the Solent makes you feel as if you are going
somewhere very special. It is a quiet, peaceful Island, far away
from the rat race. And with a strong chance of mild weather,
there is plenty of opportunity to air the lungs, stretch the legs
and enjoy plenty of sunny, winter, country walks.

Cucumber Pâté

The taste of cucumber is so refreshing. They are greenhouse grown on the Island for the mass market. I have put this recipe in the winter section as it makes a great Christmas starter

2 large, crisp cucumbers
1 tbls salt
1 oz (25gm) finely chopped mint or dill weed
4 oz (110gm) butter, softened to almost an oily state
1 tub Greek strained yoghurt or other plain yoghurt
5 fl oz tub double cream
1 sachet of gelatine crystals
lots of freshly-ground black pepper

Line the bottom of a 1 pint (570ml) terrine with greaseproof paper. Peel the cucumbers and grate. Put the grated flesh in a colander. Sprinkle with the salt and stand for 30 mins until most of the liquid has drained away. Briefly rinse under the cold tap, squeeze dry and season liberally with the black pepper.

Soften the gelatine in 2 tbls of cold water, then dissolve the crystals over a pan of simmering water. Whisk the cream to the floppy stage.

Working quickly, beat the yoghurt into the oily butter, fold in the cucumber and chopped herbs, then the dissolved gelatine. Finally, fold in the cream. Turn the mixture into the terrine and refrigerate for at least 4 hours, preferably overnight, until set.

Serve in neat slices with whole-meal toast and a few prawns to garnish. Serves 4-6.

Pheasant and Sesame Salad

2 pheasant breasts
4 tbls sesame seeds
oil for frying preferably

Dressing:
2 tbls sesame oil
4 tbls olive oil
2 tbls honeygar
1 tspn whole grain mustard
salt and black pepper

winter salad leaves
diced dessert apple

Cut the pheasant breast into strips and roll in the sesame seeds to coat. Gently pan fry the pheasant in the oil until the seeds are golden and the meat is lightly cooked.

Place the dressing ingredients in a jar with lid and shake to blend.

Arrange the winter leaves on plates with the diced apple. Arrange the cooked pheasant on top. Drizzle over the dressing and serve while the pheasant is still warm.
Serves 4 as a starter or 2 for light lunch.

Turkey Breasts with Garlic Bread Sauce

1 very large or 2 small Isle of
Wight turkey breasts
2 oz (50gm) garlic butter
1 onion, finely chopped
3 slices of crustless white bread
4 plump cloves of garlic, 1 bay leaf
pinch of nutmeg, 1 tbsp dry sherry
½ pt (275ml) milk or single cream
for a richer sauce
salt and black pepper
½ pt (275ml) giblets gravy

Smear the turkey breasts with the garlic butter and put to roast in a moderately hot oven 400°F/200°C/Gas6, for 60 mins. In a saucepan put the onion, bread (broken into pieces), whole garlic cloves, bay leaf, nutmeg, sherry and milk or cream. Simmer gently for 30 mins. Remove the bay leaf, purée the sauce, season to taste and keep warm until ready to serve. Carve the turkey which should be juicy and not dry. Arrange down the centre of each plate. Pour some garlic sauce down one side of the turkey slices and hot giblets gravy down the other side. Serve with traditional Christmas vegetables. Serves 4.

Breast of Pheasant Braised in Beaujolais

Perfect for an alternative Christmas Day lunch.

3 pheasants, dressed
2 1b (900gm) root vegetables,
peeled and cut into cubes
6 small onions or shallots,
skinned and left whole
2 tbls oil
l medium onion
2 cloves Isle of Wight smoked
garlic
1 pkt fresh mixed herbs
1 small bunch parsley
salt and pepper
6 slices of bread
1 bottle of Beaujolais (the Nouveau that you didn't drink)
1 tbls cornflour

Remove the legs, wing tips and backbone from the pheasant and place in a large saucepan with the medium onion. Cover with cold water, bring to the boil, skim then lower the heat and simmer until the meat is tender. Strain the stock and reserve. Remove the meat from the bones and blend in a food processor with salt and pepper and the mixed herbs to make a smooth paste. Reserve.

Meanwhile, put the prepared root vegetables, the onions, and the pheasant breasts that are still attached to the breast bones, in a large, deep casserole with the oil. Season with salt and lots of black pepper. Brown in a preheated oven Gas7/425°F/220°C for approx 10 mins. Pour over the wine then cover with a tight fitting lid. Reduce the oven temperature to Gas4/350°F/180°C and cook for about 1 hour until tender.

Remove the pheasant and vegetables from the casserole and keep warm. Pour the remaining liquid into a saucepan with the strained stock, thicken with the cornflour and simmer for 3-4 mins.

Toast the bread and spread with the puréed leg meat. Carve the breasts and lay over the toast. Glaze with the rich sauce. Garnish with the root vegetables and freshly chopped parsley. Accompany with small roast potatoes and Brussels sprouts. Serves 6.

83

Foraging for Mushrooms

*W*hen foraging for wild mushrooms an identification book is essential, as is a cautious nature. They say there are only two truly deadly mushrooms in this country, but that should be enough to make you check and double-check before eating them.

On top of that there are numerous species that will make you ill and even some edible ones will make a sensitive stomach revolt. The shaggy ink cap is quite delicious and makes a tasty dinner party sauce. But! if eaten with alcohol you could suffer severe palpitations and unpleasant hallucinations.

It's so easy to feel romantic about foraging for mushrooms, but if there is any doubt in your mind then leave well alone. Instead buy your wild fungi at a local delicatessen where they are picked and packed by experts.

Having said that, parasol mushrooms are easy to recognize and can be found in abundance during the autumn. However, a wide variety of mushrooms can be purchased in many shops on the Island. Fresh oyster mushrooms have a good flavour and delicate texture. Serve either raw in salads or quickly toss in hot oil. Fresh shitake mushrooms have a milder flavour but a more robust, meaty texture and look good sliced in casseroles.

Some of the best mushrooms are the large locally-grown, open-capped mushrooms which provide a good, dark, strong flavour to dishes.

Dried mushrooms do seem to be expensive, yet they have such a powerful flavour only a few are required to elevate a simple mushroom dish to something quite outstanding.

The most common varieties are morels and ceps and half an ounce is sufficient to enhance the flavour of a pound of cultivated mushrooms.

Soak dried mushrooms in a basin of hot water and stand for 3-4 hours (or cold water and stand in the fridge overnight). Morels tend to carry bits of grit and sand in their folds, so once they are swollen remove from the water and strain the liquid through a fine sieve. Retain the liquid and use as stock.

A popular dish from the kitchen of Gods Providence House

Townhouse Pie

3 lb (1.4kg) mince beef (we use Isle of Wight beef)
2 onions - finely chopped
1 lb (½ kg) mushrooms - finely chopped
2 tbls of Italian herbs
1 pint (570ml) water
½ (275ml) pint of red wine
gravy mix
creamed potatoes

Place all ingredients into an ovenproof dish, except the cream potatoes. Cover with foil.

Bake in oven, Gas4/150°C/300°F for 2 hours.

Remove from oven, mix, then thicken with gravy mix. Return to oven for 20 mins. Place into individual dishes.

Top with cream potatoes. Grill until golden brown. Serve with freshly cooked vegetables.

Christmas Ice-Cream

Several small farms are now producing ice cream on the Island. Minghella's ice cream is our most famous but there is also the very good ice cream from Calbourne Classics and Chale Farm. This recipe shows you how to make your own without the aid of an ice-cream maker.

1 pt (570ml) double cream
4 oz (110gm) castor sugar
2 eggs, separated,
4 tbls rum
2 oz (50gm) glacé cherries,
1 oz (25gm) angelica
1 oz (25gm) candied peel
1 oz (25gm) lightly toasted flaked almonds
1 oz (25gm) chopped pistachio nuts
2 oz (50gm) sultanas,
1 tspn mixed spice
grated rind and juice of 1 orange
grated rind and juice of 1 lemon
½ tspn vanilla essence

Chop the glacé cherries and angelica into tiny pieces. Put the sultanas, orange juice and rind, lemon juice and rind and the rum in a bowl. Leave to soften overnight.

Put the egg yolks and castor sugar in a bowl and whisk over a pan of simmering water until pale and creamy. Cool.

Whisk the cream with the mixed spice until thick. Fold in the cold egg yolk mixture, the nuts, chopped fruits and the fruit softened in the rum mixture and all the liquid.

Whisk the egg whites until stiff, then fold into the cream mixture. Turn into a pudding basin that has been lined at the bottom with a piece of greaseproof paper. Cover and freeze until ready to serve.

To serve, quickly dip the pudding basin in hot water to loosen the sides and turn out onto a plate. Serve with spicy Island honey sauce, recipe page 76
Serves 6-8.

Little Pots of Chocolate

Nick and Nicola Hayward created the highly acclaimed Seaview Hotel, now under new ownership, but still very good. They always had this delicious dessert on their sweet menu.

10 oz (275 gm) plain Bournville or darker chocolate
1 pt (570 ml) single cream
1 oz (25 gm) castor sugar (optional)
3 tbsp dark rum or coarse brandy
1 sachet of gelatine (1 level teaspoon removed)
1 oz (25 gm) butter

Melt the chocolate in a basin over a saucepan of simmering water. Be very careful not to let any moisture touch the chocolate.

Put the cream and sugar in a saucepan and sprinkle over the gelatine. Stand for a couple of minutes until the gelatine has swollen. Heat gently until the gelatine has melted and the sugar dissolved. Add the melted chocolate to the cream and stir thoroughly. Take off the heat and add the rum. Pour into ramekin dishes or pretty cups. Cool, then chill in the refrigerator. Serve with a dollop of whipped cream and a sweet strawberry. Makes about 6.

Three courses from the kitchen of The Fighting Cocks

Pea Soup

1 lb (500gms) frozen peas
2 pts (1.1ltr) chicken stock
2 oz (50gm) butter
2 oz (50gm) plain flour
1 chopped onion
1 punnet mint

Cook the butter and flour together in a pan over a low heat to make a roux. Add the chicken stock gradually, stirring all the time until the required consistency. In a separate pan sweat off the onions until tender, add to the soup with the peas. Return the soup to the boil. Liquidize the soup, season to taste, and add mint before serving. For a more chunky soup only liquidize half of the soup.

Fish Pie

2 1b (900gm) mixed seafood of your choice
1 glass white wine
1 white onion chopped
1 lb (500gms) sliced mushrooms
4 oz (110gm) butter
4 oz (110gm) plain flour
½ pt (275ml) milk
½ pt (275ml) double cream
chopped parsley
2 lb (900gm) potatoes
4 oz (110gm) cheese

Gently poach the fish in a shallow tray with some of the cream, milk, onion, and seasoning (try not to boil). When the fish starts to crumble take it out of the liquid and leave to cool.

Make a roux with the flour and the butter. Gradually add the liquid from the fish along with the rest of the milk, cream and wine. Simmer until the liquid thickens, add the fish and some chopped parsley.

Cook the potatoes for the mash adding some butter, seasoning, and some cheese to taste.

Place the fish mixture into a pie dish top with the mash potato and cook in the oven until brown on top.

Raspberry Crème Brulée

1 lb (500gms) frozen/fresh raspberries
1 pt (570ml) milk
1 pt (570ml) double cream
6 egg yolks
vanilla essence
8 oz (225gm) caster sugar
1 tbls of cornflour or custard powder

Place the egg yolks in approx ⅓ of the liquid, add the sugar, cornflour, and vanilla essence. Heat the remainder of the liquid until almost boiling. Add the egg yolk mixture to the hot milk/cream. Return to a low heat stirring continuously. When the mixture coats the spoon remove from the heat.

Place the raspberries into shallow dishes, pour on the heated egg/milk mixture. Place the shallow dishes in a tray of water and bake in the oven, very low for approx 45 mins until set. Leave to cool in the fridge. Sprinkle with sugar, brown under grill until the sugar is caramelised and serve.

The Isle of Wight Dough-nut

*H*ow the Island became famous for doughnuts is a mystery but it has been mooted that the Isle of Wight dough-nut was referred to in history books as far back as the 17th century.

More recently, in her 1845 edition of Modern Cookery for Private Families, Eliza Acton lists a recipe that has been used ever since. Jane Grigson a well-known 20th century cookery writer also thought it worth a mention in her splendid book about British foods.

There was a time when the dough-nut was so popular on the Island that every baker's shop and teashop had its own special recipe. And it was once considered the done thing after a visit to Newport on market day to pop into Westmore's dough-nut shop for a cup of tea and a dough-nut.

There are numerous varieties of dough-nuts, but the Isle of Wight dough-nut has special requirements. First of all it has to be nice and greasy, having been cooked in lard, and very stretchy. But most important of all is that it contains currants and mixed peel. Finally they aren't supposed to be very big, the size of a tangerine is about right.

These traditional cakes can still be bought in a few shops scattered around the Island.

Original Isle of Wight Dough-nut

This recipe has been in Mrs Gache's family since 1908 when her family owned the Joliffe pie shop in Newport.

1 lb (450gm) plain white flour
2 oz (50gm) lard
2 oz (50gm)castor sugar
1 oz (25gm) fresh yeast
½ pt (275ml) luke warm water
4 oz (110gm) currants
1 oz (25gm) diced candied peel
pinch salt

Blend the yeast with the water, add the sugar, stir in and leave until frothy

Mix together the flour and salt and rub in the lard. Add the yeast liquid and mix to a soft dough. Add the dried fruit. Knead until smooth then leave in a warm place to rise to double its size.

Knead again on a floured board and divide into 12 pieces. Mould into round balls the size of a walnut and leave to rise for a further 30 mins.

Heat oil in a deep saucepan until hot. Fry the doughnuts quickly until golden brown. Drain and toss in castor sugar.

Patsy Gache, who has been a baker all her life, says the sign of a good doughnut is its crisp, greasy outer coating, and its stretchy insides.

Try Mapes Bakery in Sandown for a huge range of dough-nuts

Victoria Sandwich

4 oz (110 gm) butter
4 oz (110 gm) castor sugar
2 eggs
4 oz (110 gm) self-raising flour
few drops of vanilla essence

Cream together the butter and sugar until soft, pale and fluffy. Beat in the eggs one at a time, adding a tspn of flour with each egg if there are signs of curdling. If the butter is soft enough this shouldn't happen. Beat in the vanilla essence. Sift the flour and gently fold into the mixture.

Lightly oil and flour two 6 inch sandwich tins and divide the mixture evenly between both. Level out the mixture then make a small shallow hollow in the centre.

Bake in a preheated oven 375°F/190°C/Gas Mark 5 for 20-25 minutes. When cooked, turn out and cool on a wire rack. Sandwich together with raspberry jam. These days strawberry or apricot jam or lemon curd are also used and even fresh whipped cream for a more luxurious Victoria Sandwich.

Queen Victoria's Sweet Tooth

Queen Victoria spent many months each year at her holiday home Osborne House, and it was well-known that she had a sweet tooth and a passion for fresh fruit. Although she was an advocate of seasonal food and always insisted that the best of the season was always on her table even if she never had any—it simply gave her pleasure to see it there—when it came to fruit she seemed to waive this rule. She had several forcing (hot) houses, melon grounds and fruit rooms installed so that she could be supplied with exotic fruit all the year round. Some of her favourites were oranges, grapes, pears and monster apples.

During the summer months she insisted that her luncheon table was always graced with wild strawberries from the woods, (still to be found today), and grapes and raspberries from her kitchen garden.

From the kitchen of the Quay Arts Café

Date Oatie

10 oz (275gms) dates
6 oz (175gms) margarine
4 oz (110gms) brown sugar
10 oz (275gms) oats

Heat the dates in a microwave covering them with hot water. Heat until they are a 'mush'. Add more hot water if they are too dry. In another pan melt the margarine. Add the sugar. When the mixture is hot add the oats. Mix together well. In a rectangular tin already lined, put in half the oat mixture and spread flat. Add the date mixture and spread over the oats. Add the remaining oat mixture over the dates and press firmly. Bake in a pre-heated oven for approx 30 mins. Gas4/170°C/325°F. Cut into squares while still warm.

Vegan/Vegetarian/Nut free/Dairy free/Gluten free
Makes 5 portions

92

From the kitchen of the Steephill Cove Beach Café

Cherry and Coconut Flapjacks

Preheat oven to Gas Mark 3/4 (moderate)/160°C (fan)/180°C (convection)

9 oz (250gm) butter
5 oz (150gm) golden syrup
5 oz (150gm) soft light brown sugar
3 oz (75gm) desiccated coconut
11 oz (320gm) porridge oats
7 oz (200gm) glacé cherries

Place the butter, syrup, and sugar in a saucepan and warm over a medium heat until the butter has melted and sugar dissolved, stirring occasionally. Once this has happened increase the heat and let the mixture bubble for a few minutes. Turn off heat. Add this to the oats, cherries, and coconut. Mix thoroughly.

Using a small tray bake tin, or whatever tin you have, eg 8 inch round cake tin, lined with greaseproof paper or tin foil that has been greased, pack in the flapjack mixture and level out. Place in the oven for about 30 mins until light golden brown.

Remove and leave to stand for 5 mins, then cut into the size portions required and leave the flapjacks to cool in the tin—this may take about an hour or so. Then eat and enjoy!

Conversion Tables

All these are approximate conversions which have either been rounded up or down. In a few recipes it has been necessary to modify them very slightly. Never mix metric and imperial measurements in one recipe; stick to one system or the other.

WEIGHTS		VOLUME		MEASUREMENT		
½ oz	10 gm	1 fl oz	25 ml	¼ inch	0.5 cm	
1	25	2	50	½	1	
1½	40	3	75	1	2.5	
2	50	5(¼ pint)	150	2	5	
3	75	10(½)	275	3	7.5	
4	110	15(¾)	400	4	10	
5	150	1 (pint)	570	6	15	
6	175	1¼	700	7	18	
7	200	1½	900	8	20.5	
8	225	1¾	1 litre	9	23	
9	250	2	1.1	11	28	
10	275	2¼	1.3	12	30.5	
12	350	2½	1.4			
13	375	2¾	1.6			
14	400	3	1.75			
15	425	3¼	1.8	OVEN TEMPERATURE		
1 lb	450	3½	2	Gas 1	275F	140C
1¼	550	3¾	2.1	2	300	150
1½	700	4	2.3	3	325	170
2	900	5	2.8	4	350	180
3	1.4 kg	6	3.4	5	375	190
4	1.8	7	4	6	400	200
5	2.3	8 (1 gal)	4.5	7	425	220
				8	450	230
				9	475	240

INDEX

INDEX